Engage in the enjoyable therapeutic relaxation of colouring. Designed by hypnotherapist Liz Stewart, gently unwind your mind, reduce stress and boost mental clarity with these beautiful illustrations and patterns to create a healthy peaceful calm wherever you are.

Designed for use with any art medium, printed 1 image to 1 page sheet for crisp, clear results.

Hypnotic Colouring meditations can be found at www.enjoyconfidence.com including audio tracks for Confidence, anxiety release, weight loss and relaxation to enhance your enjoyment and benefits.

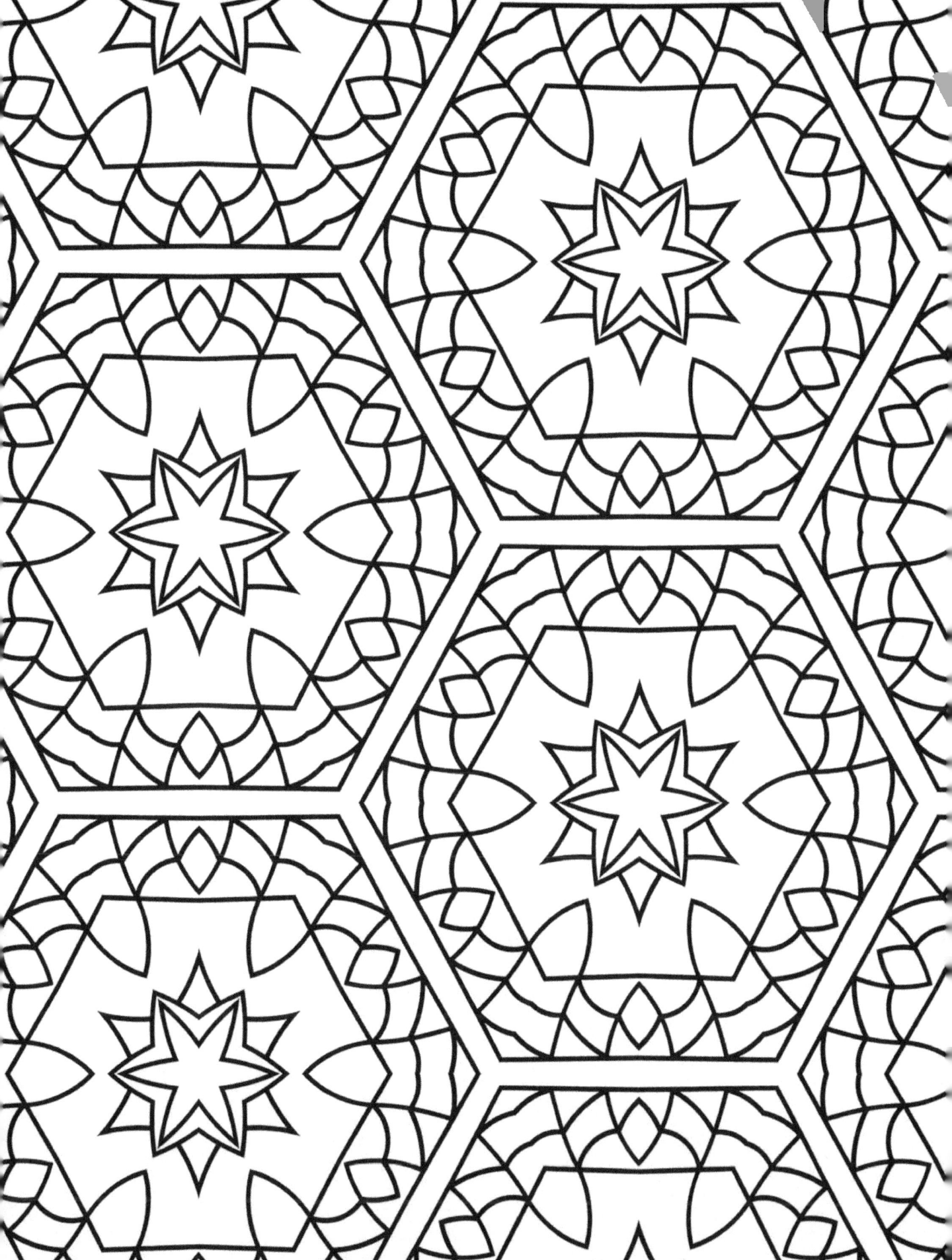

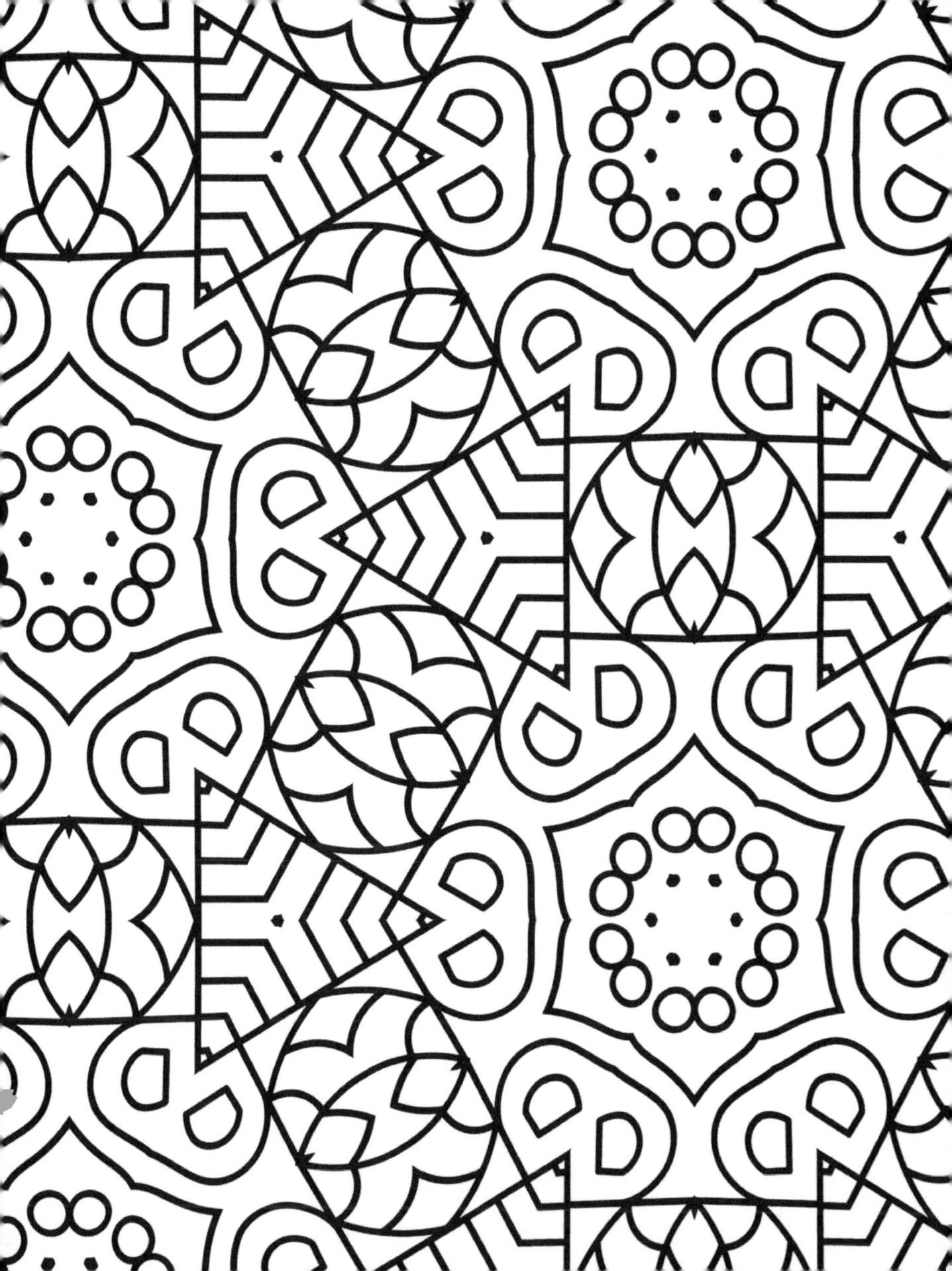

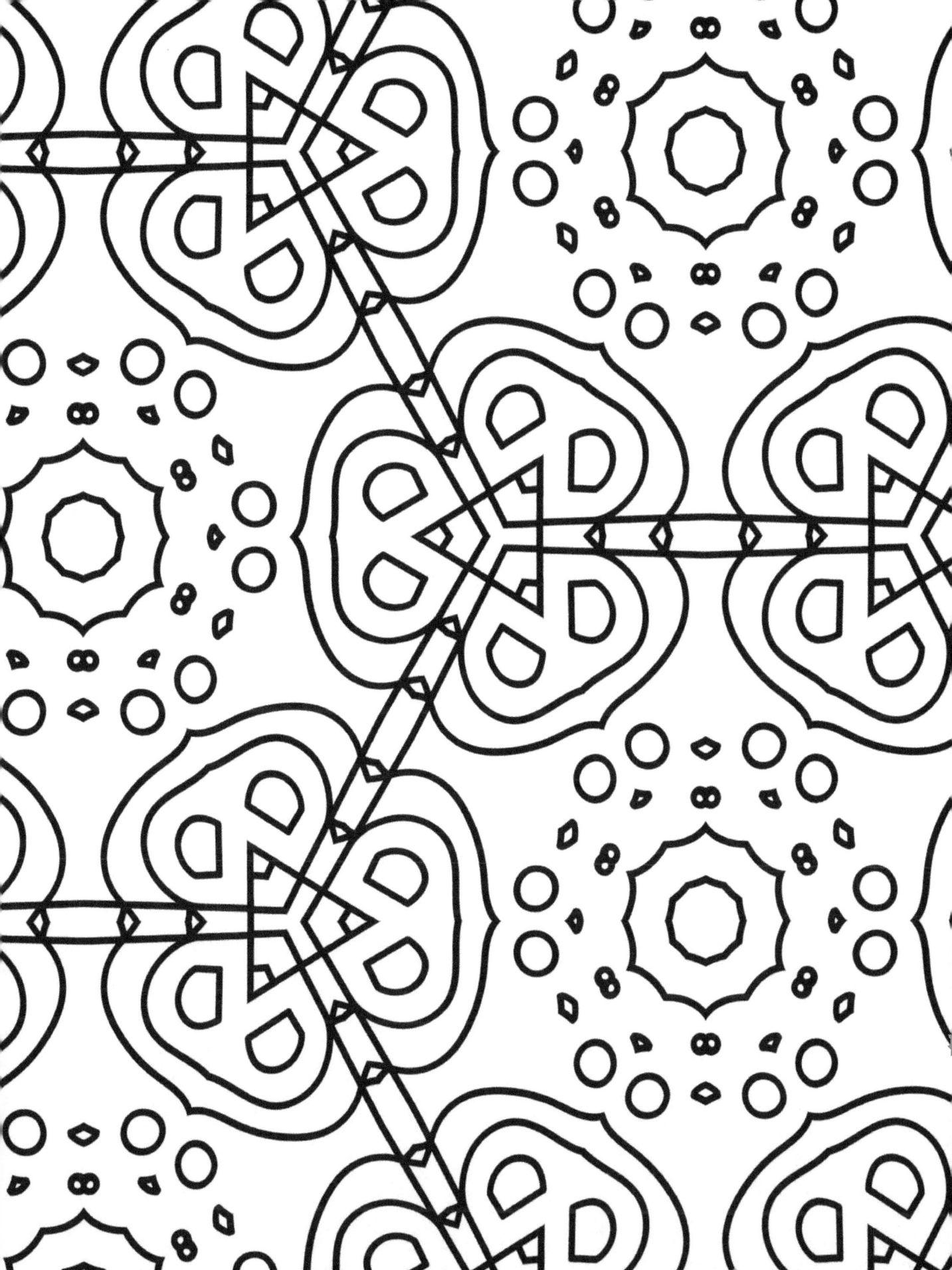

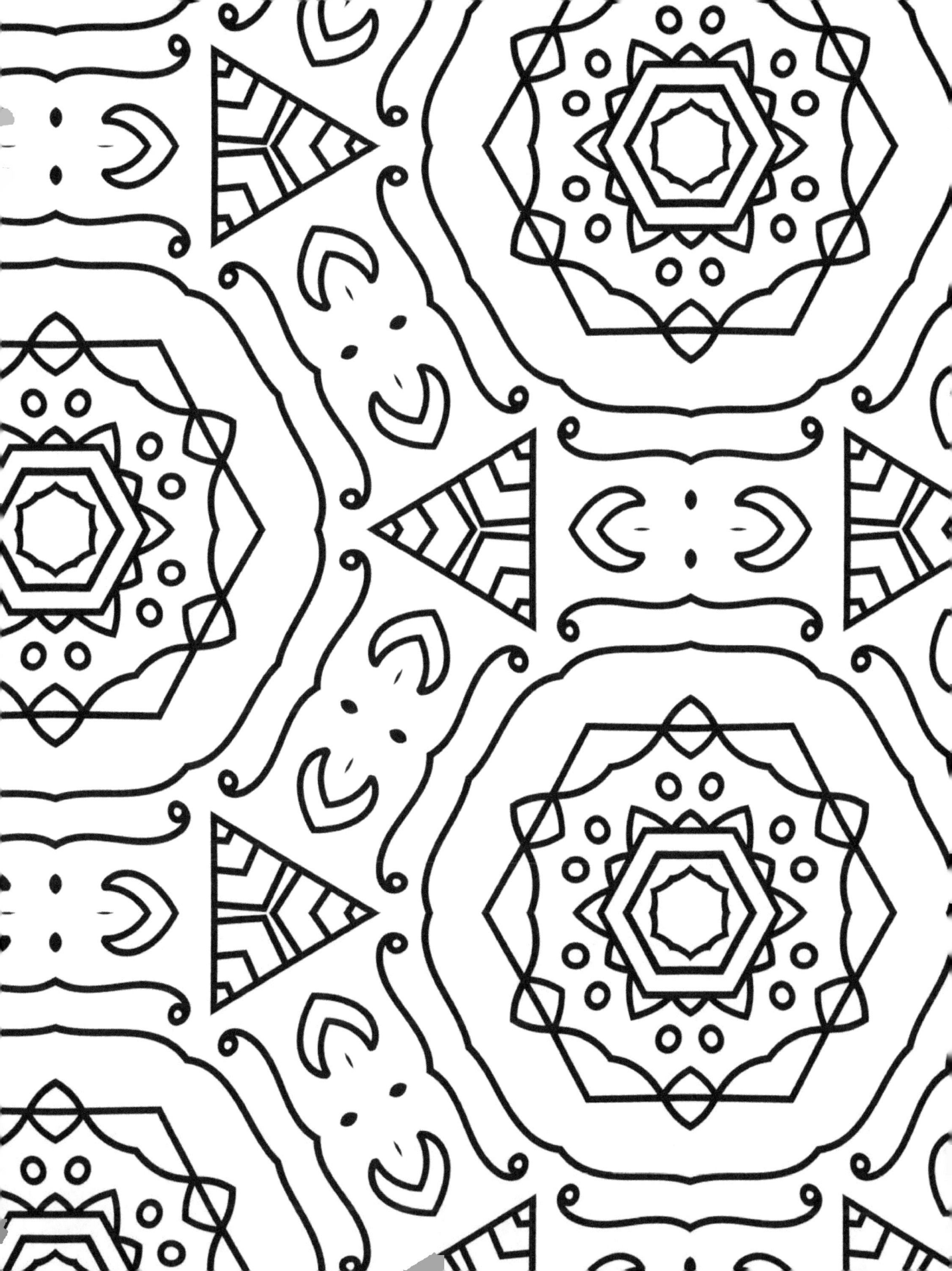

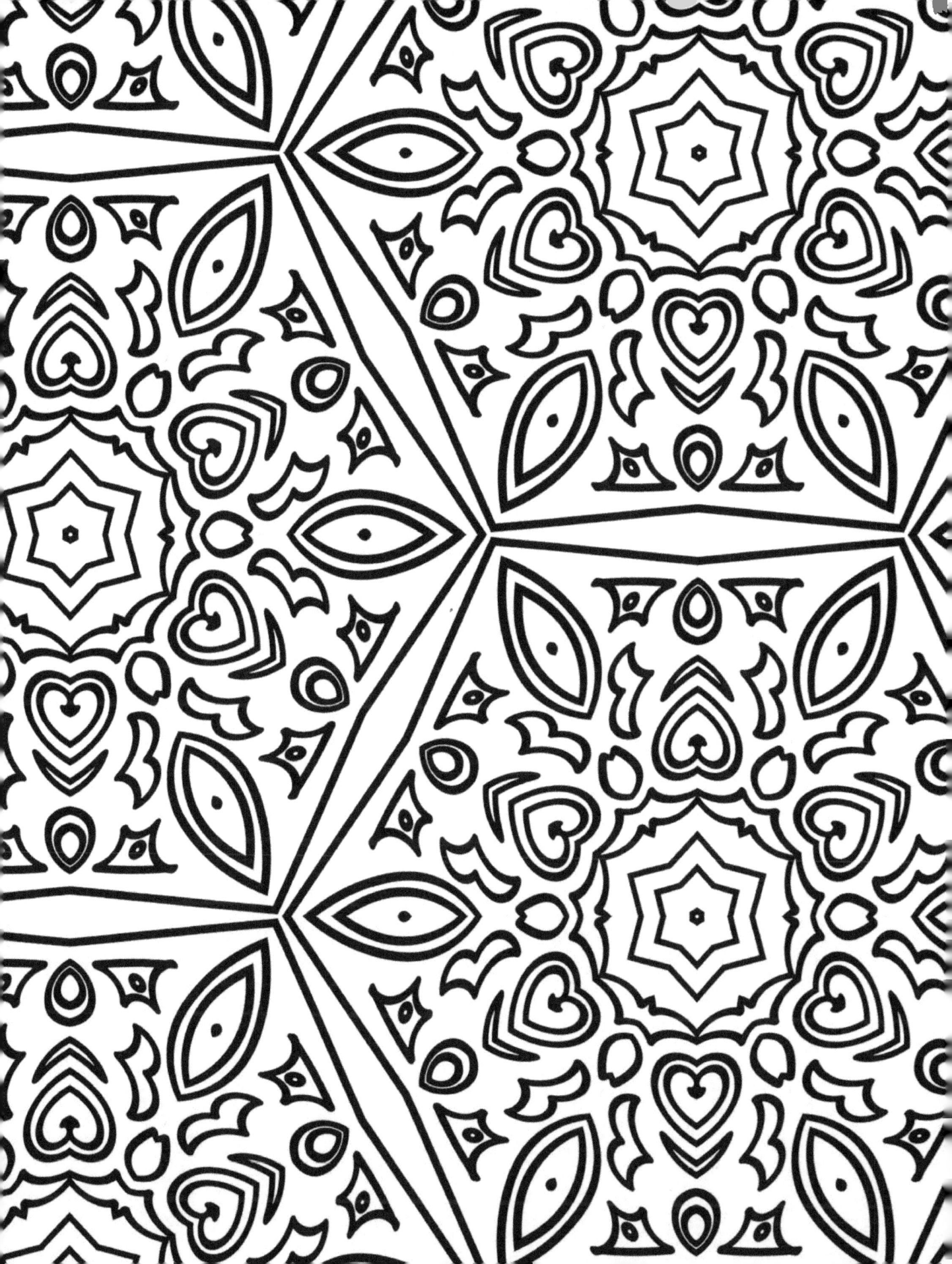

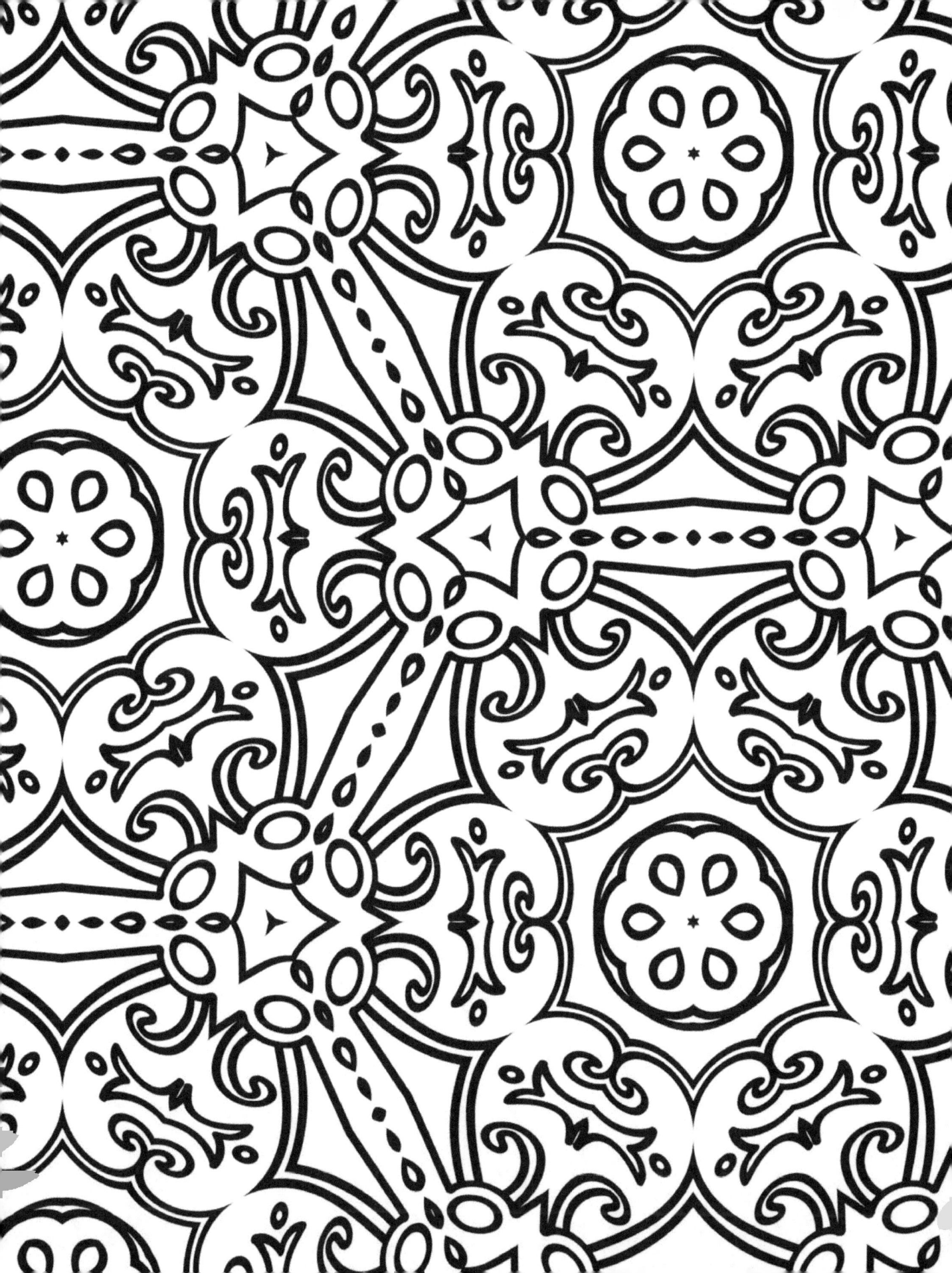

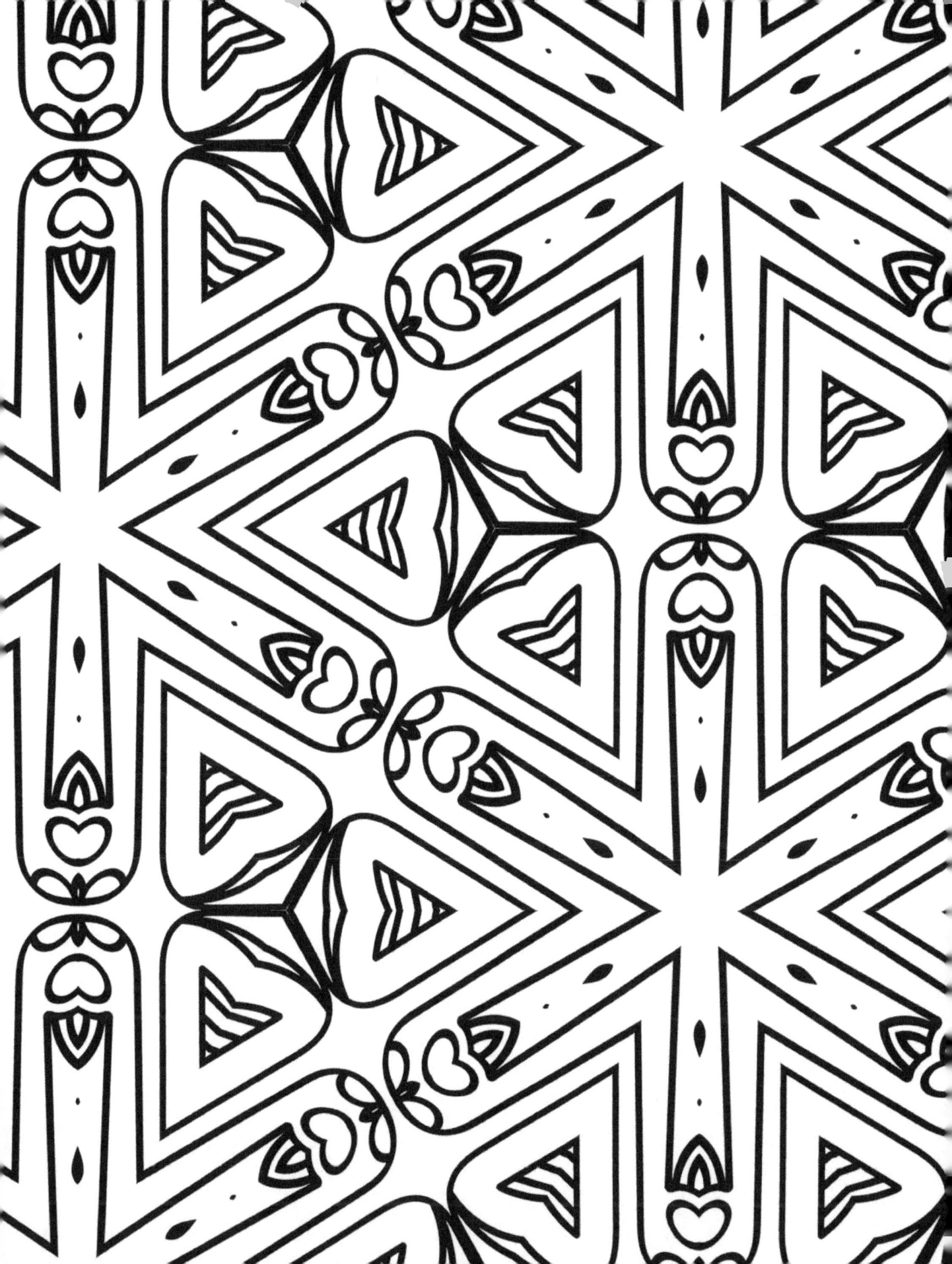

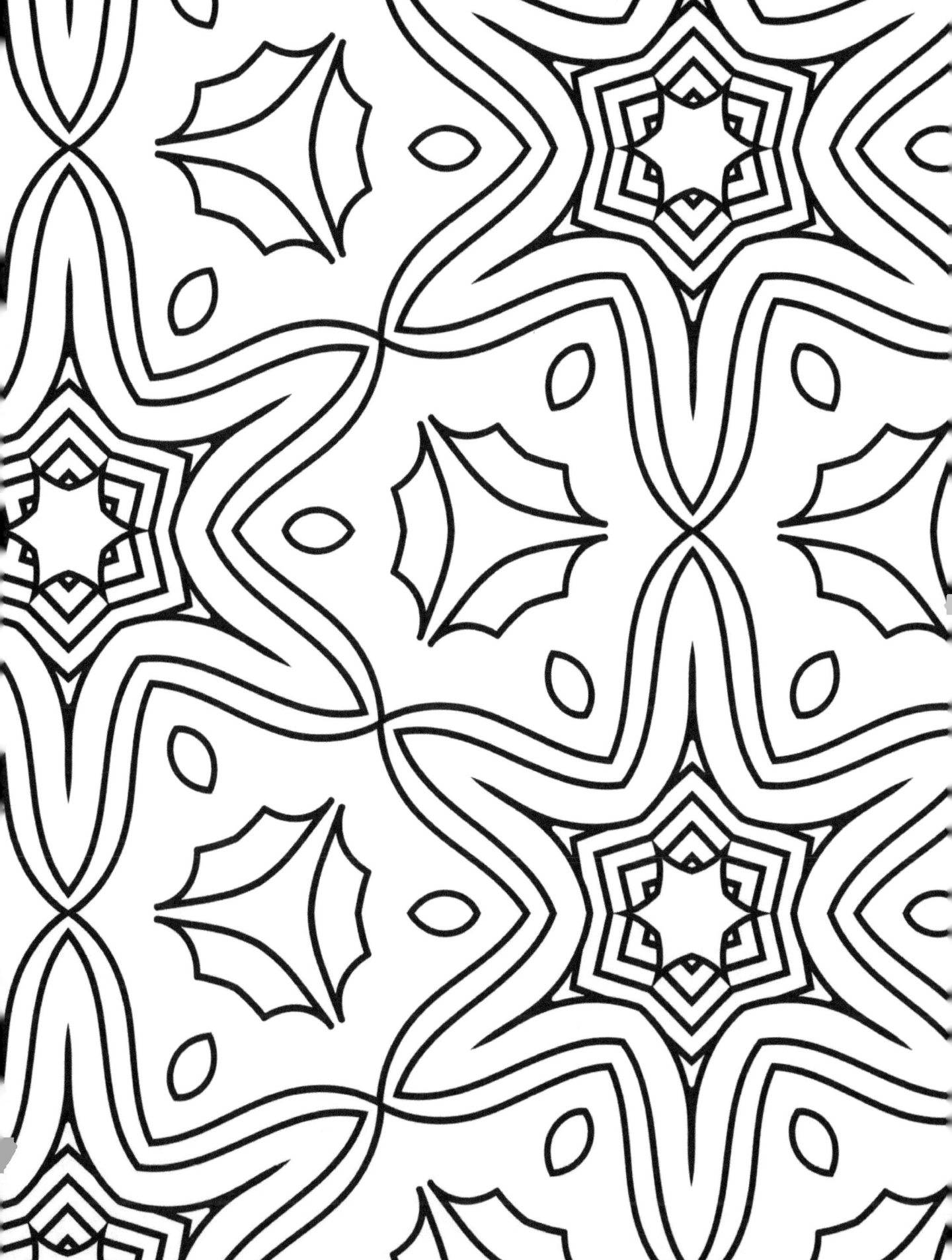

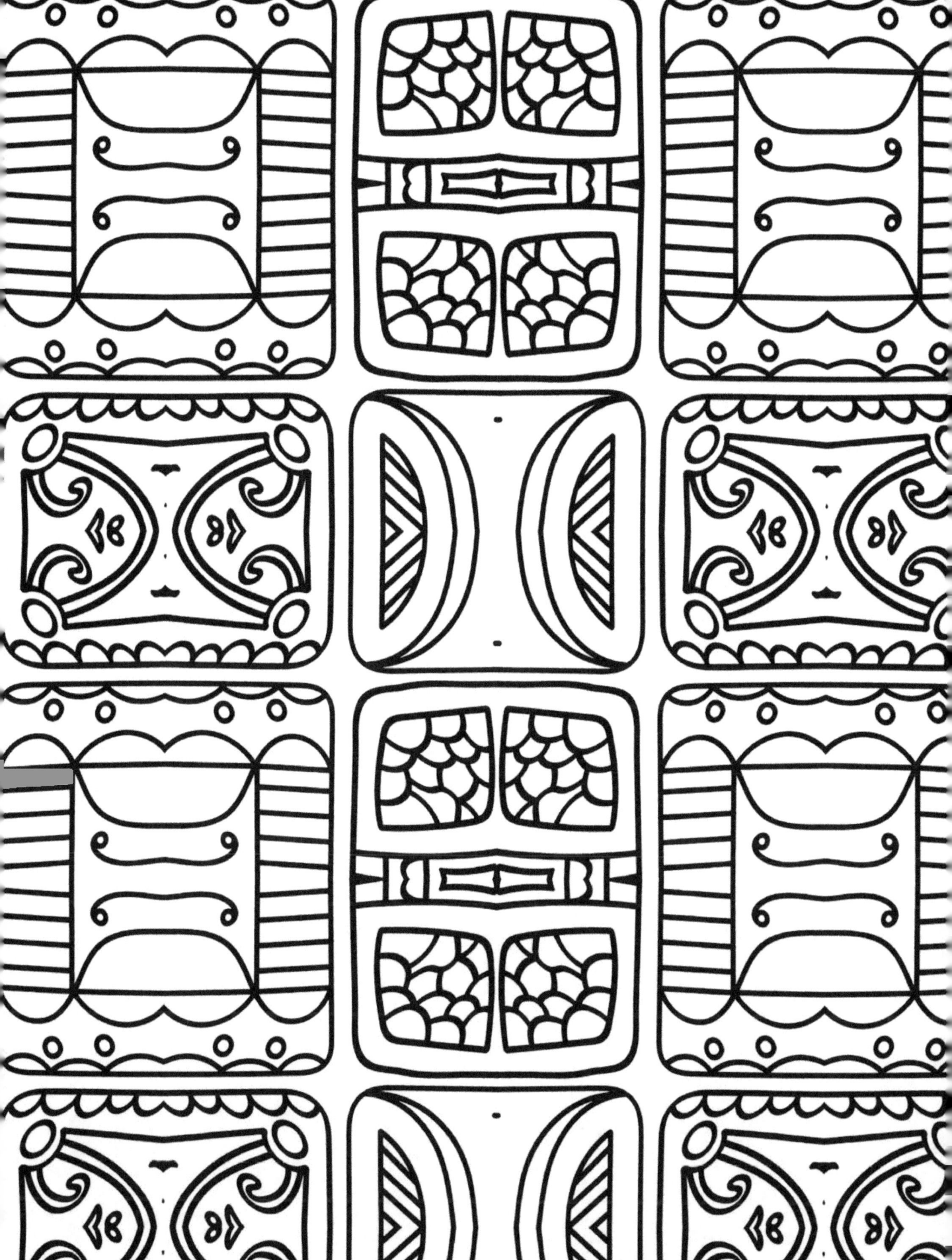

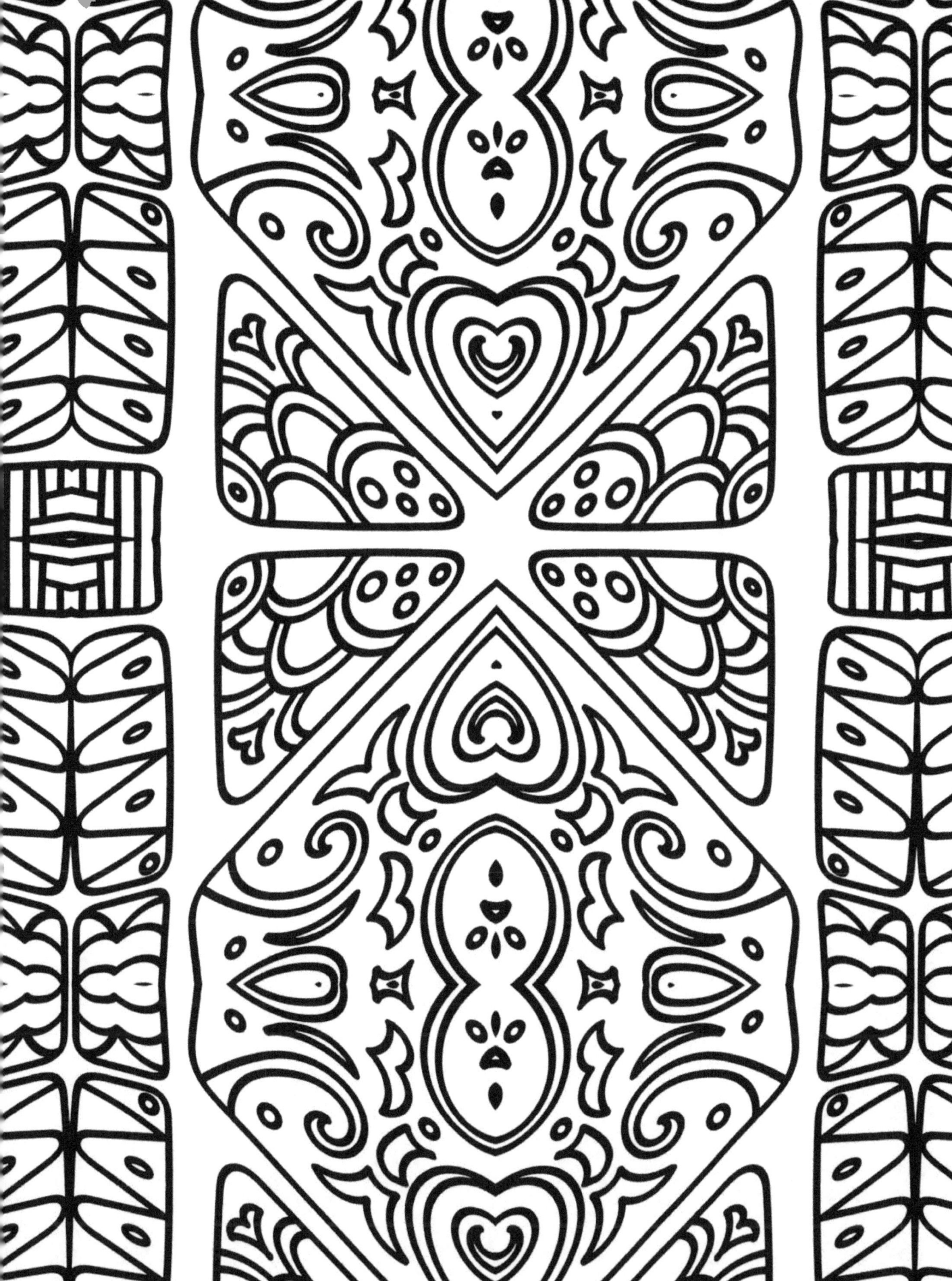

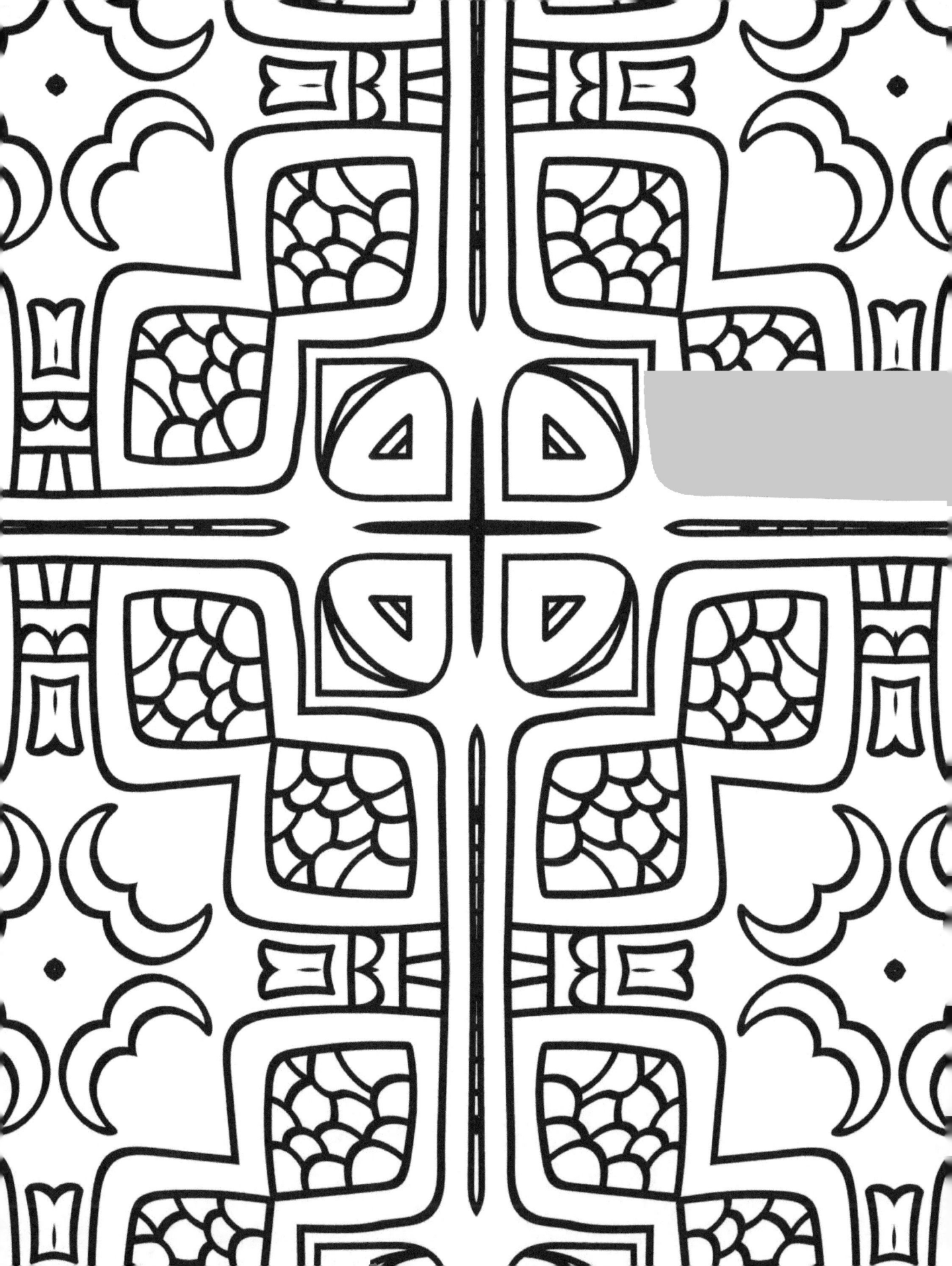

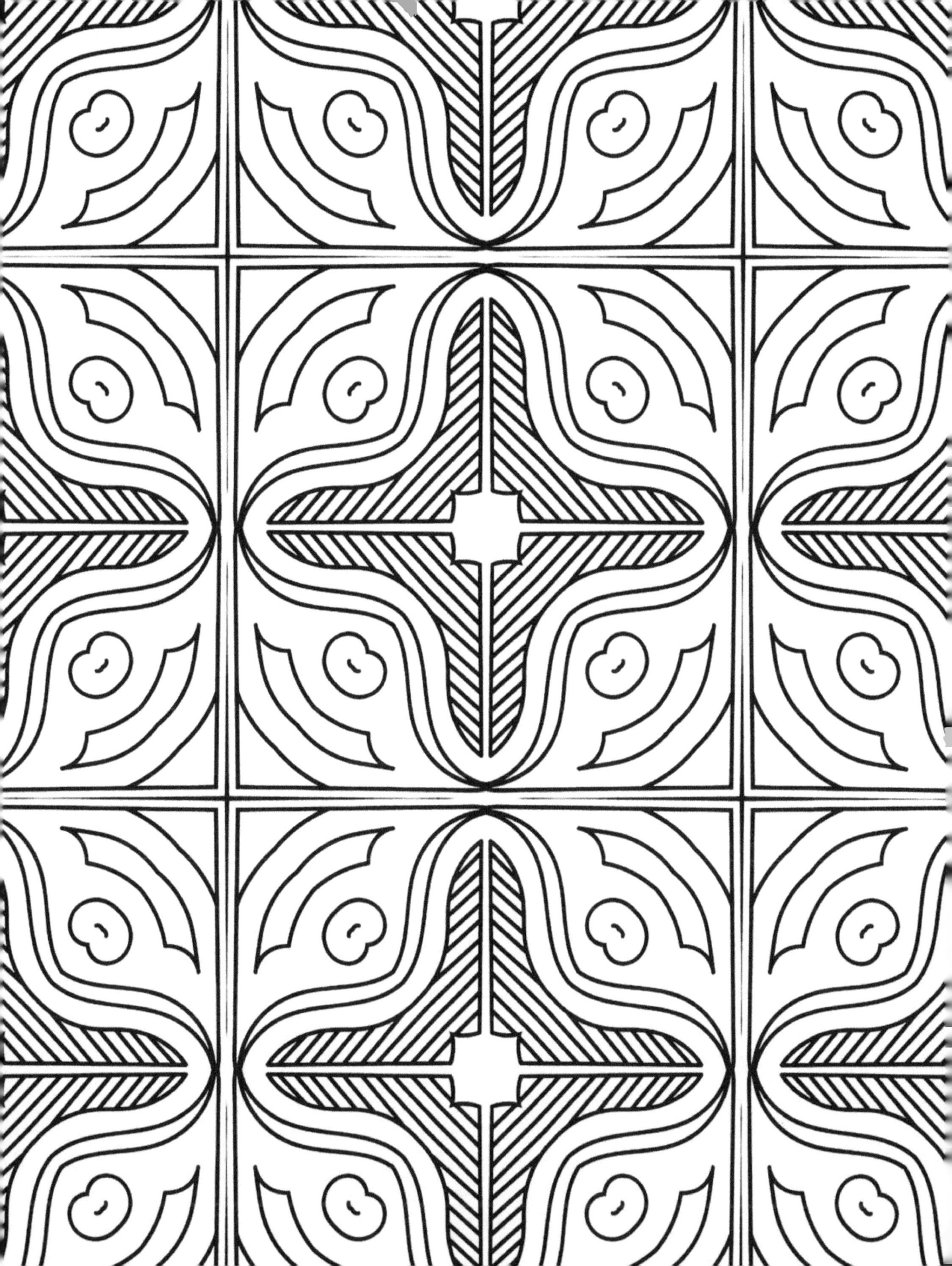

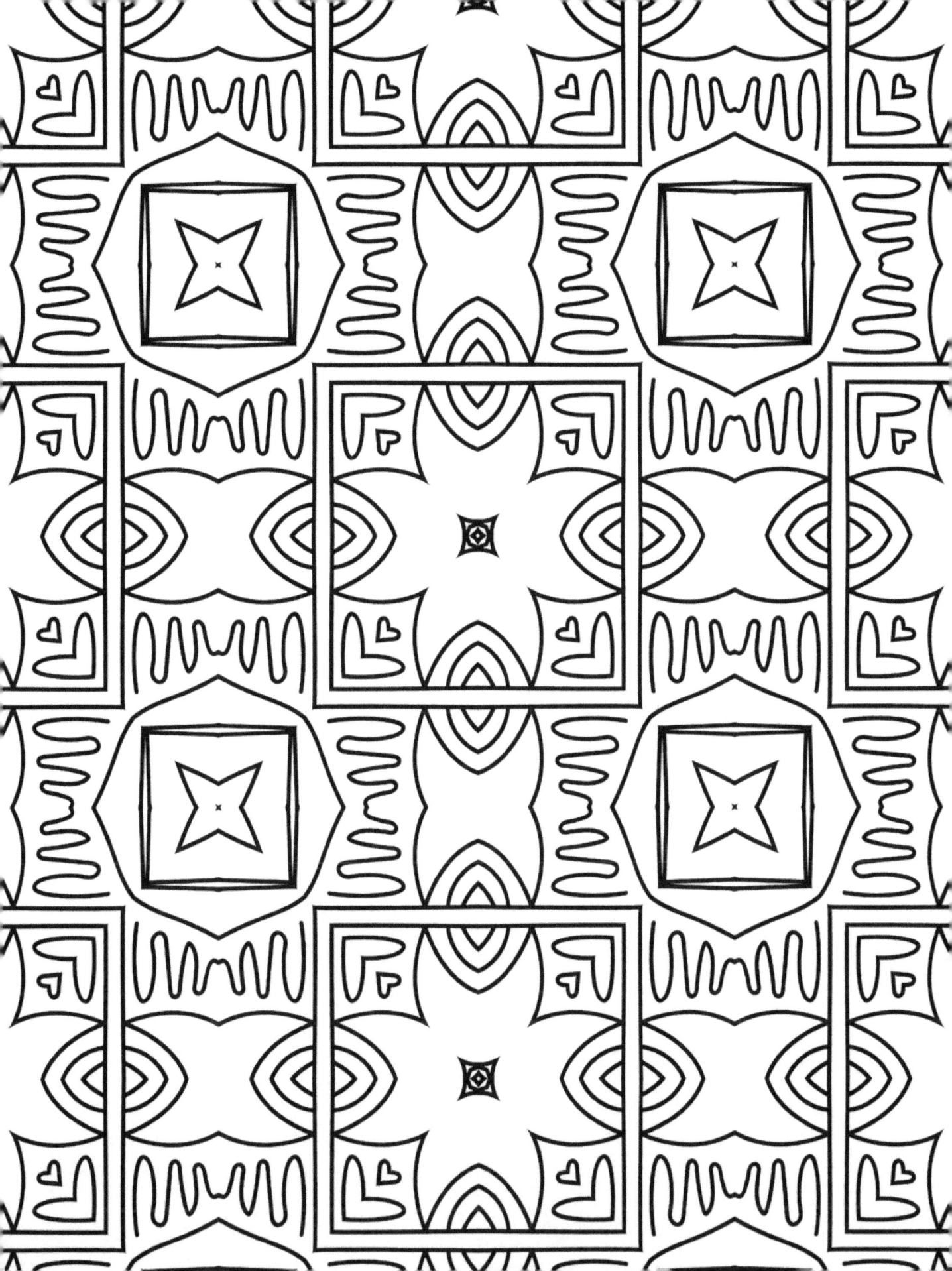

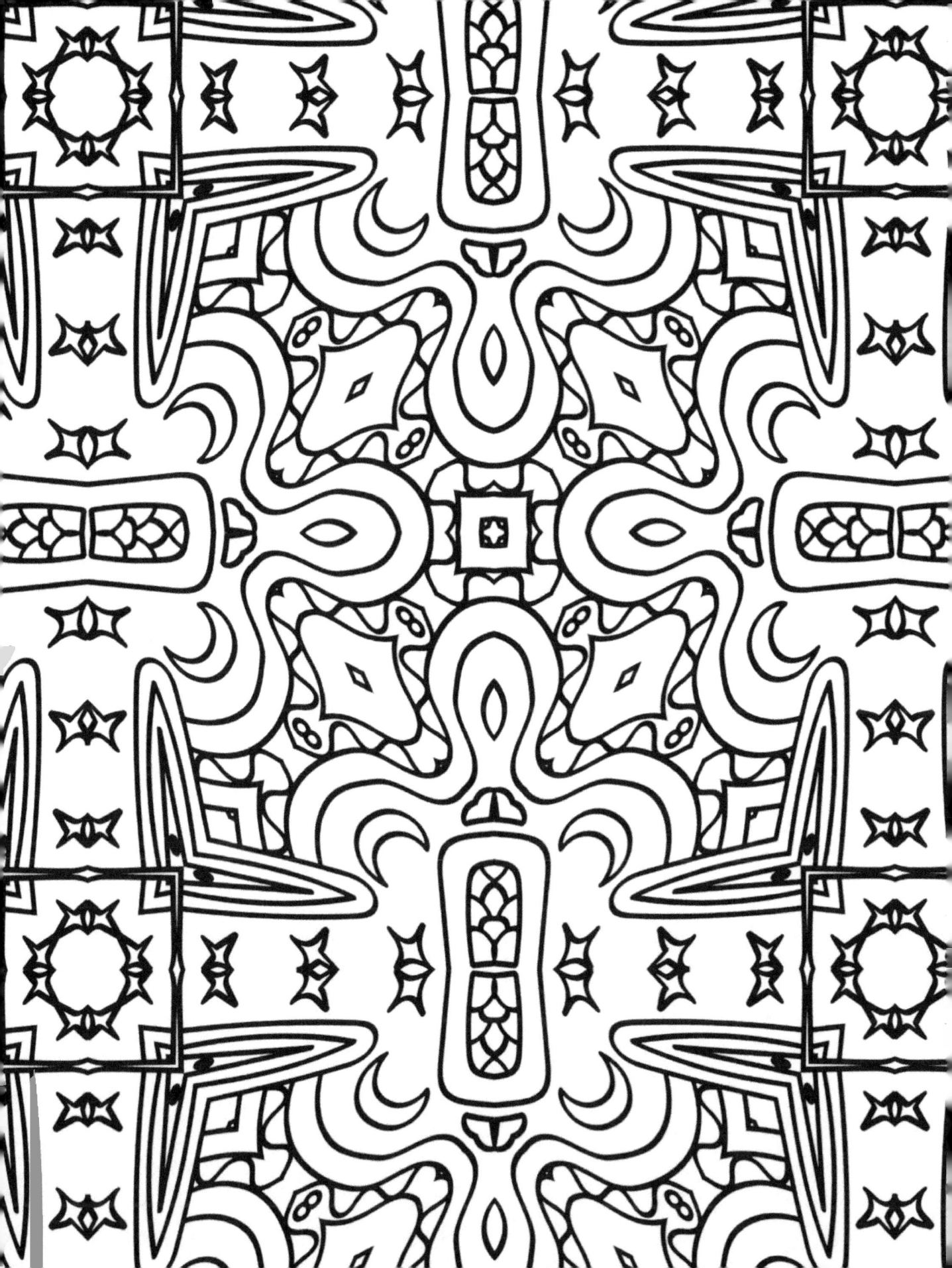

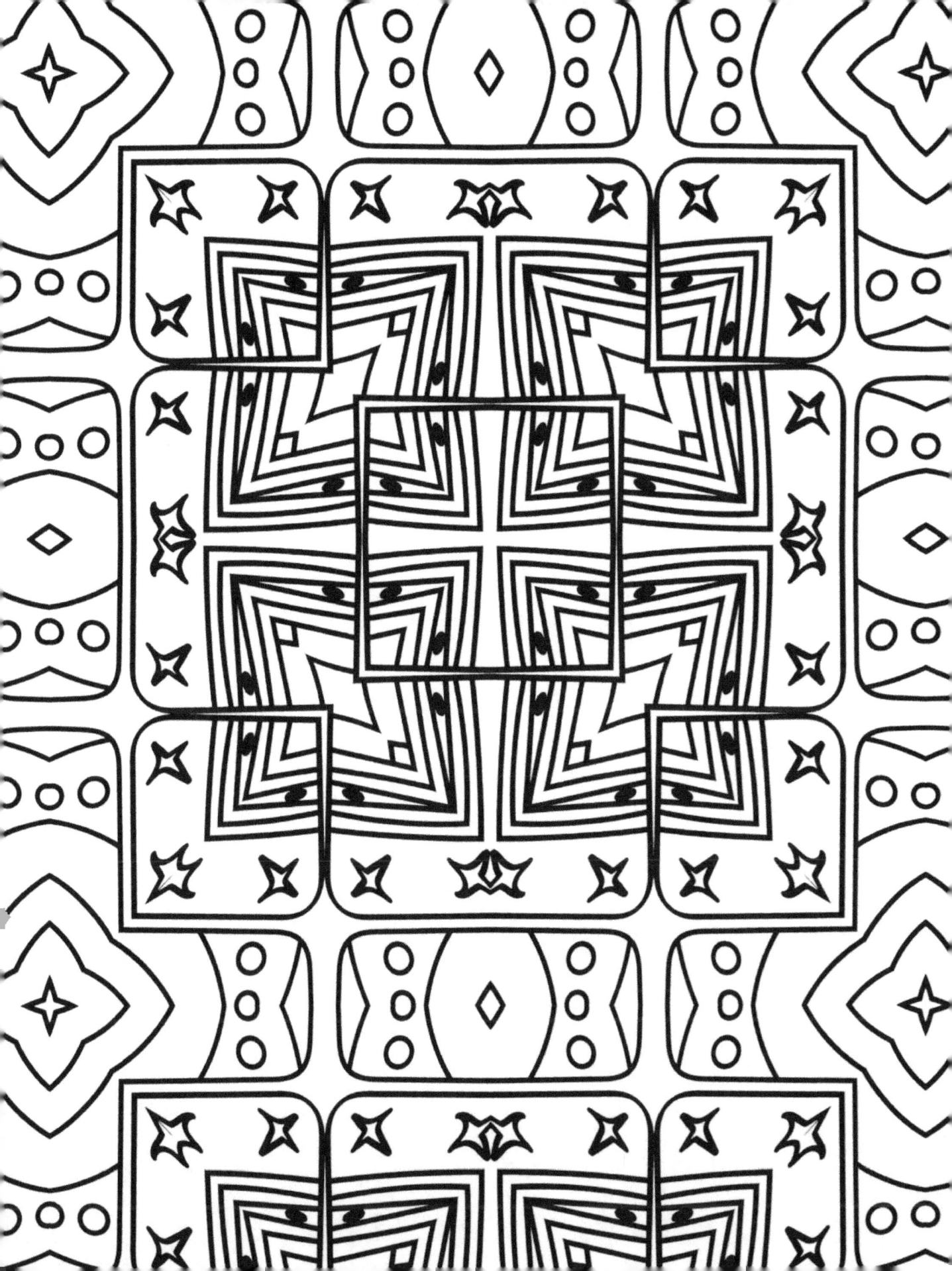

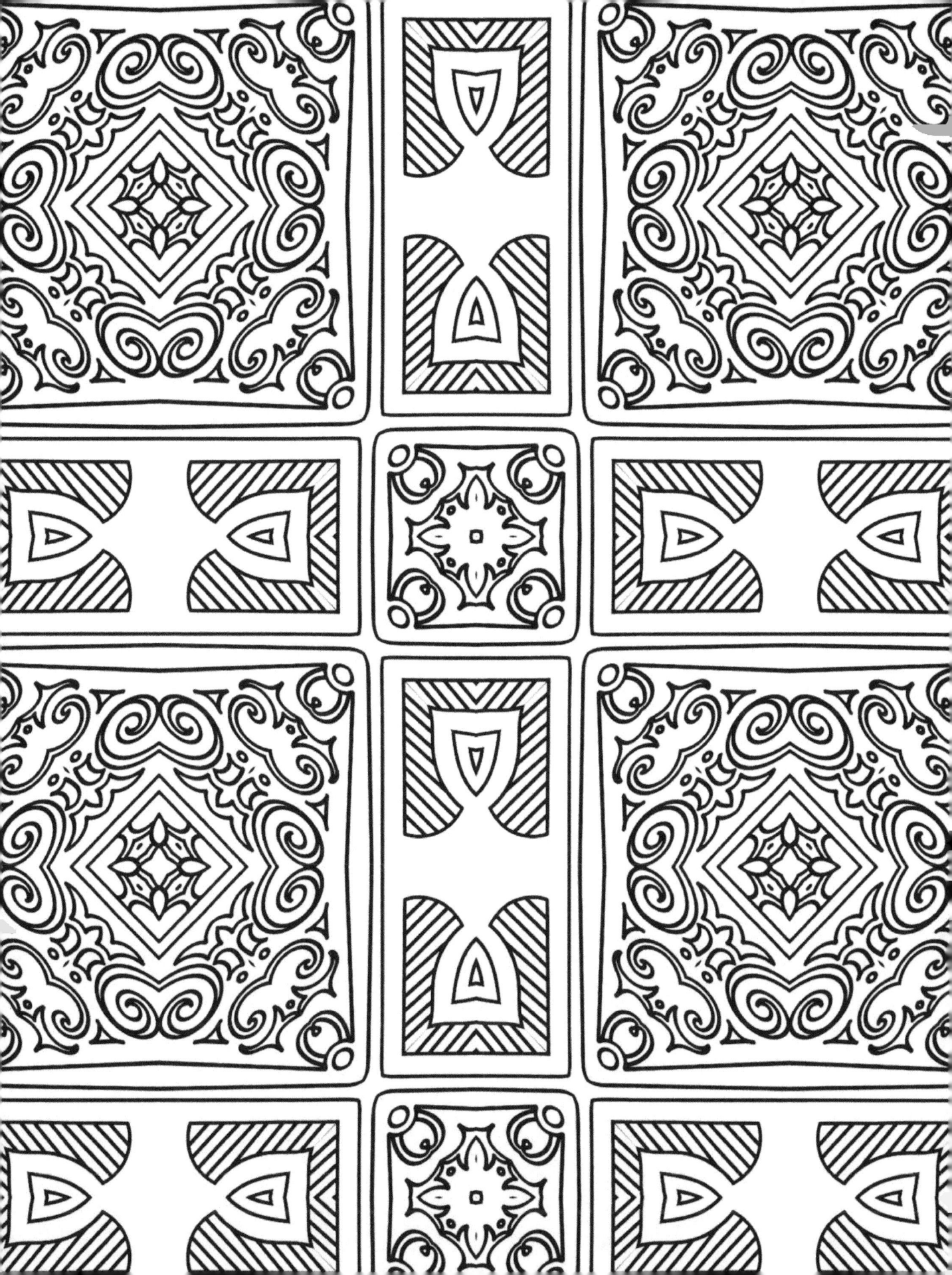

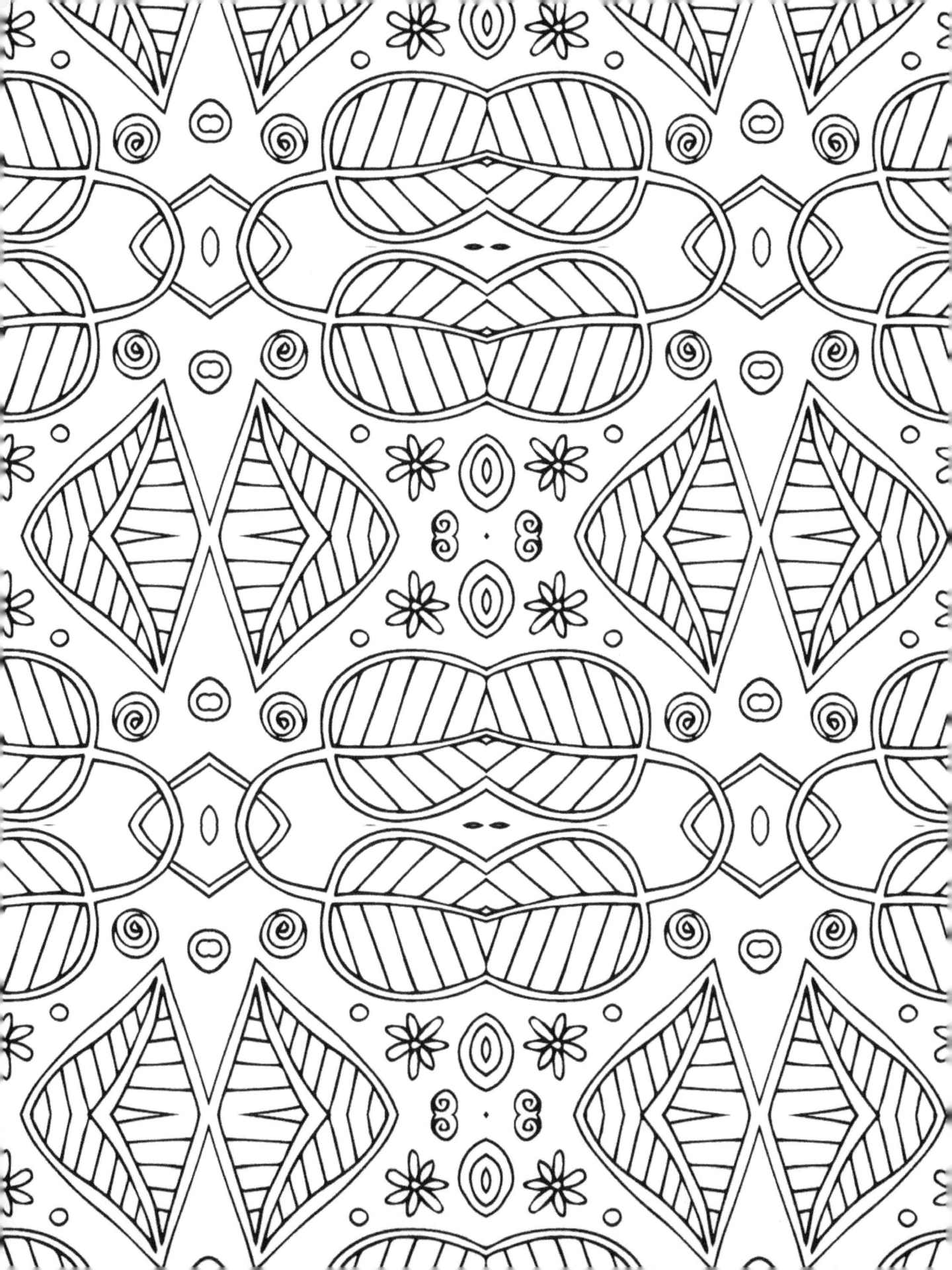

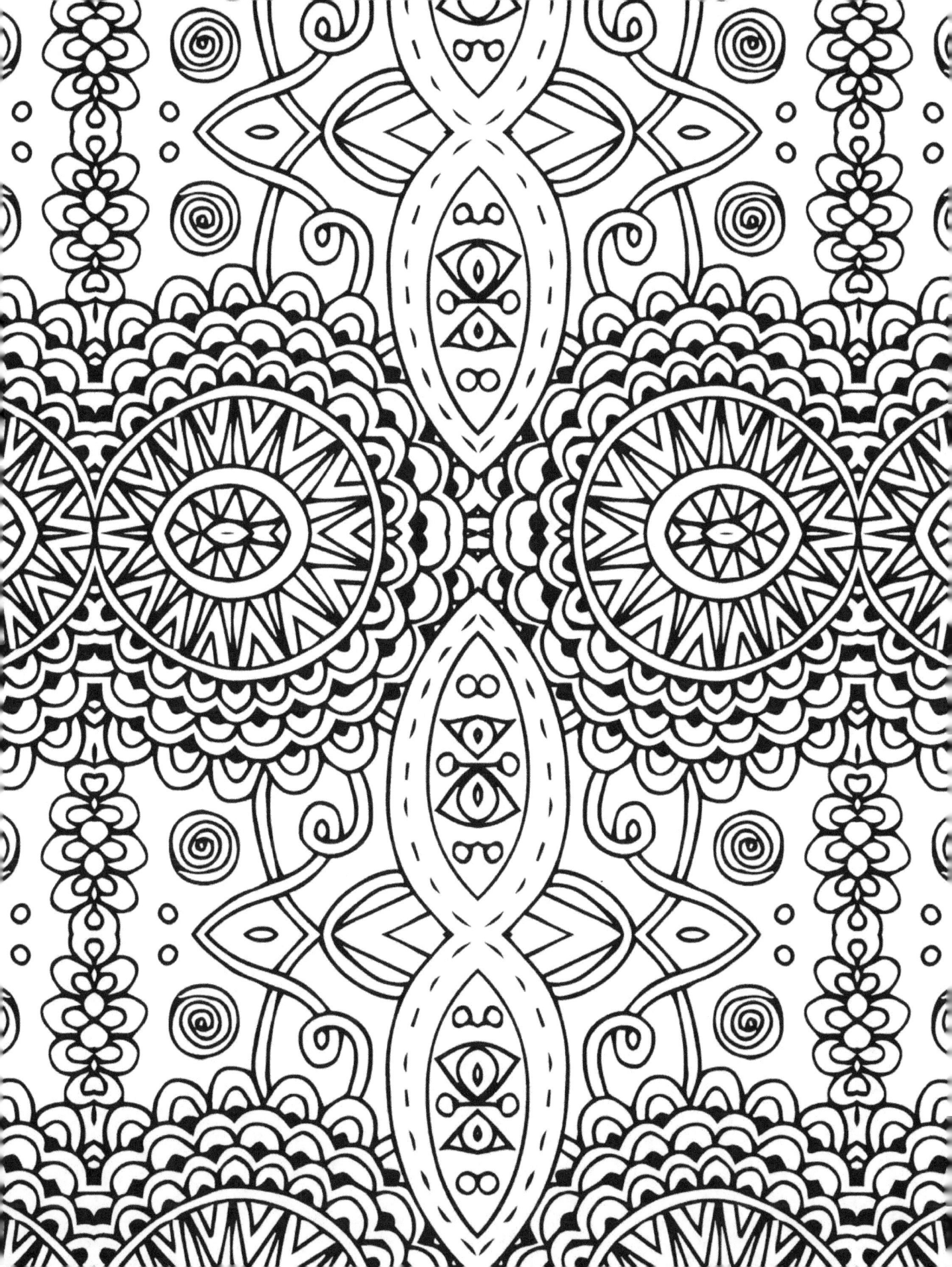

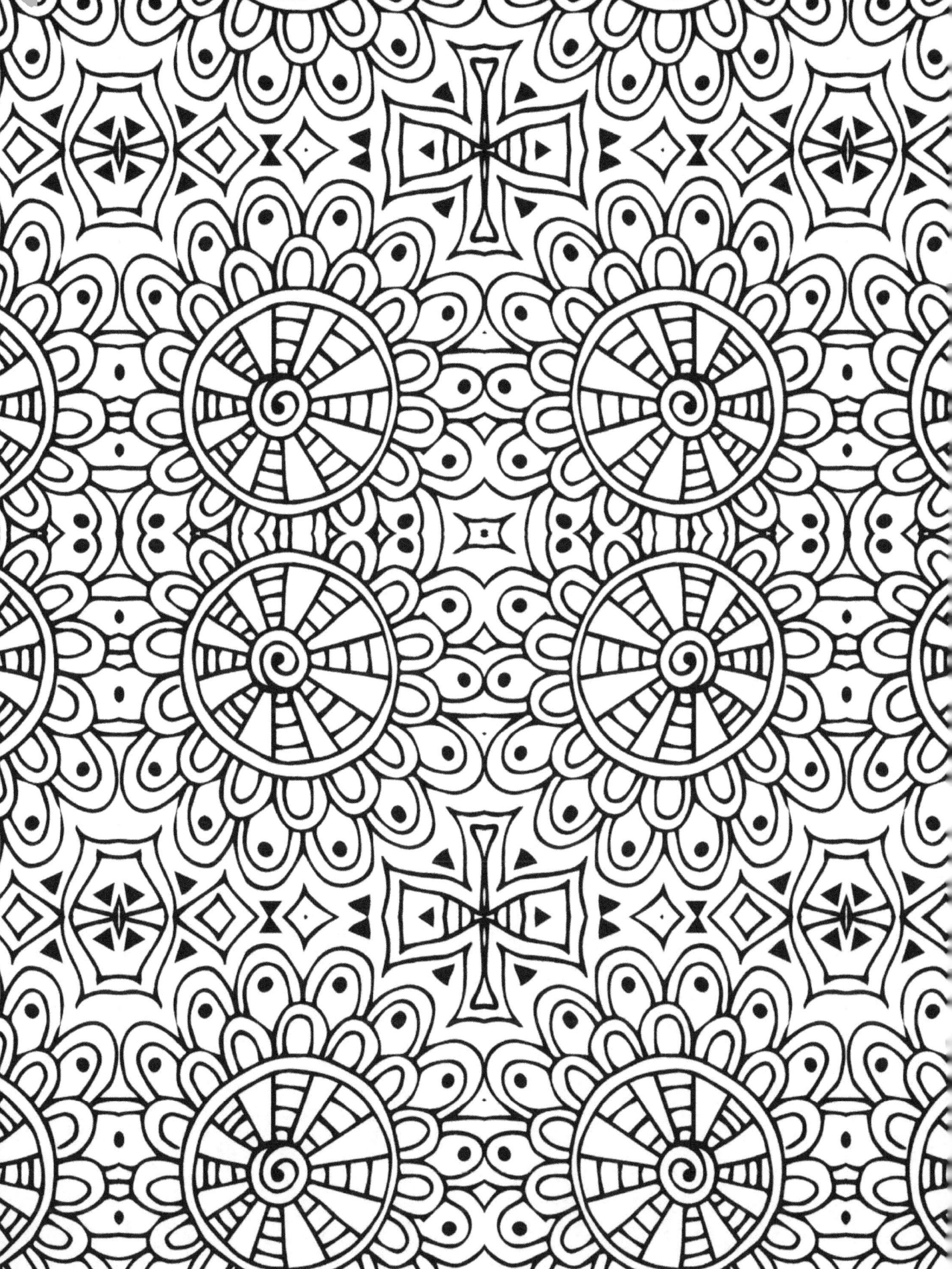

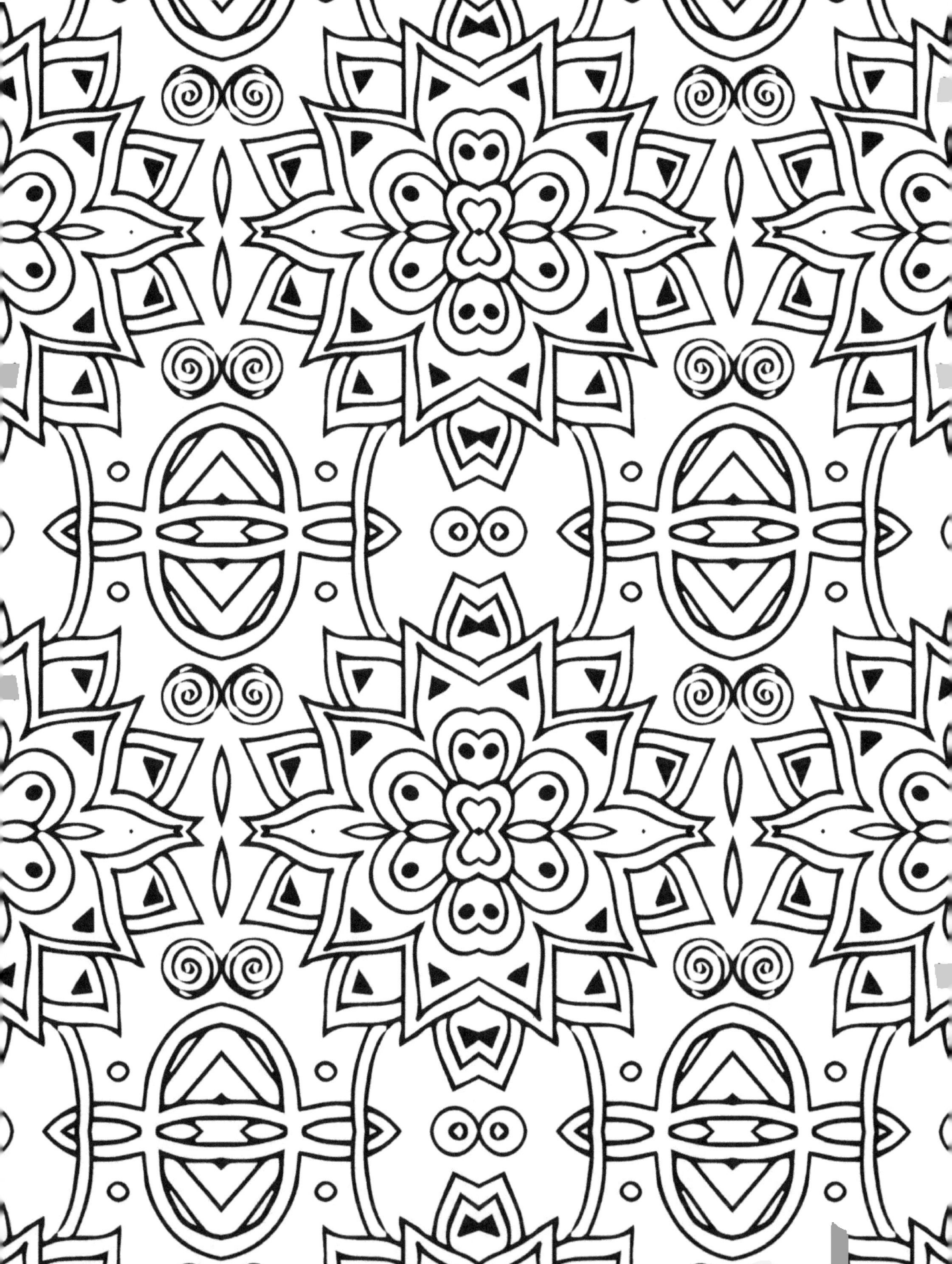

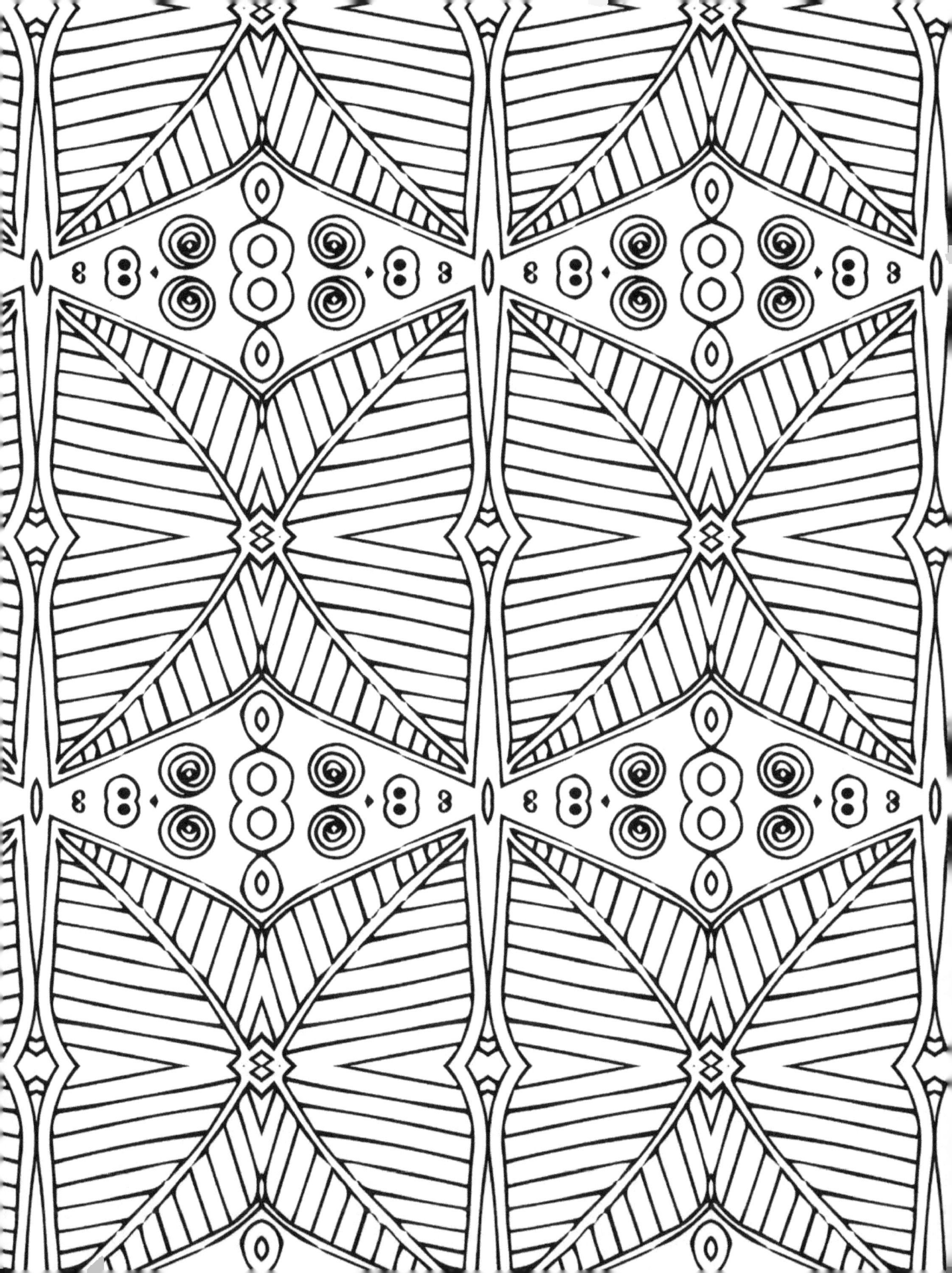

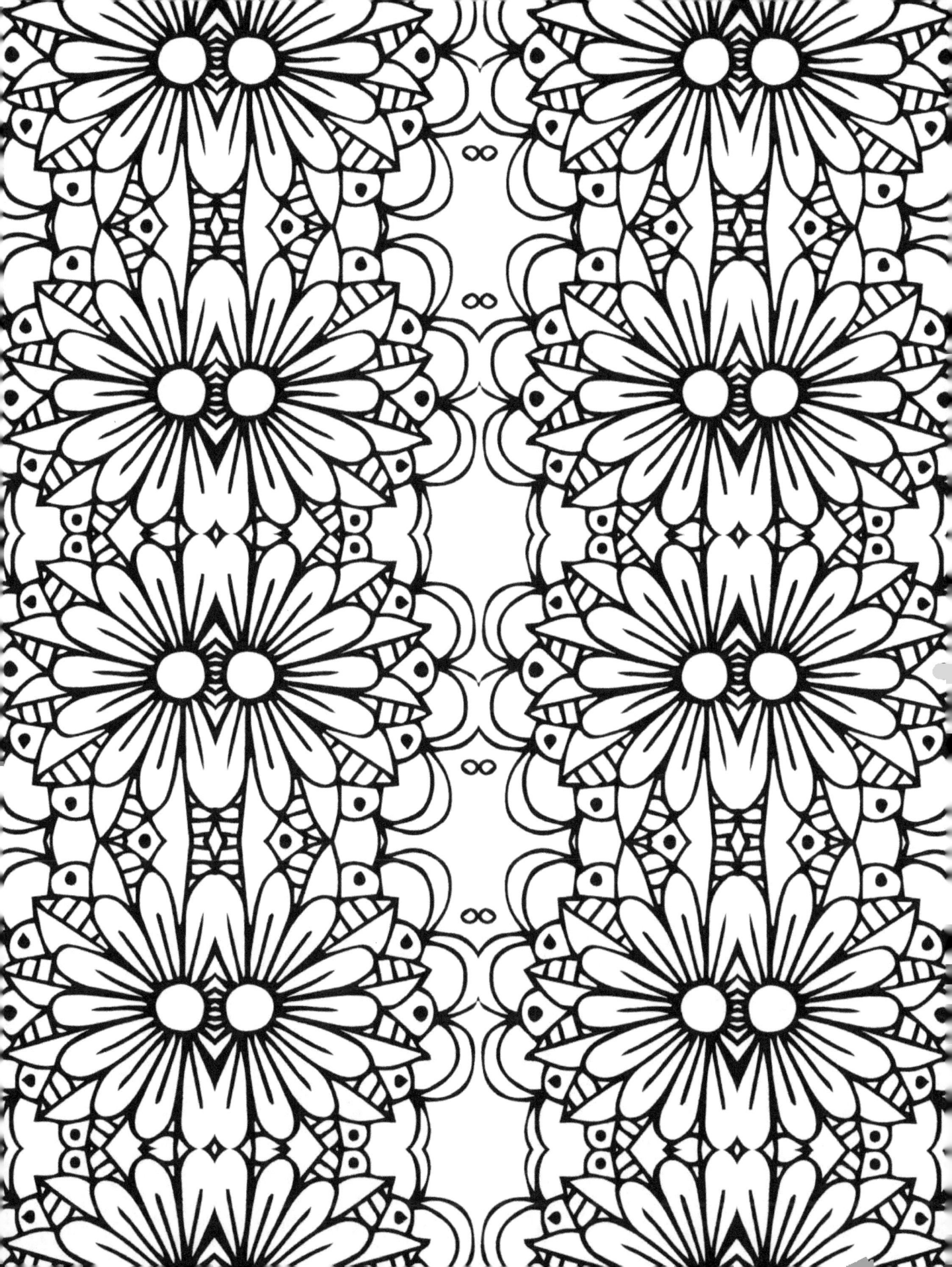

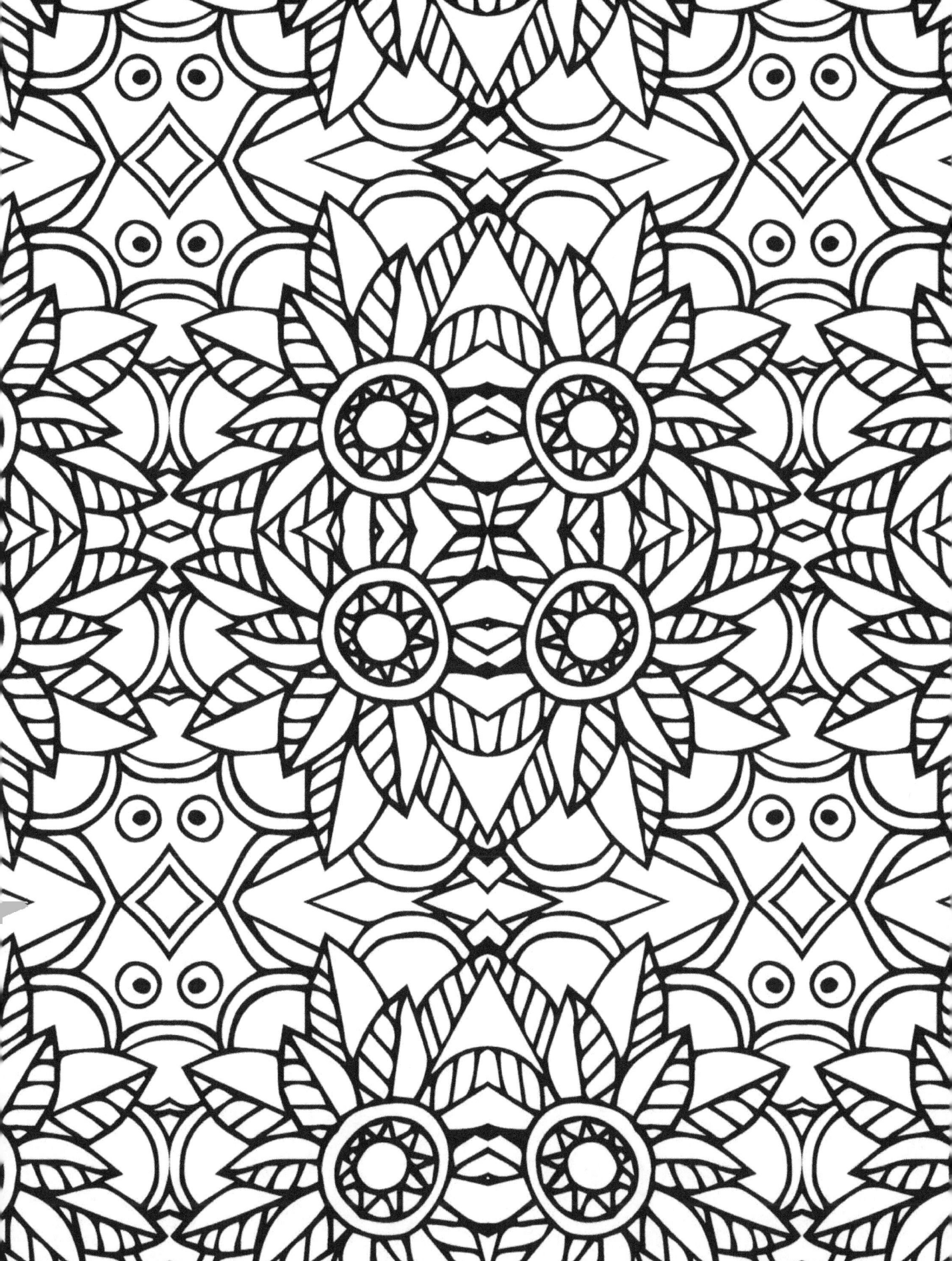

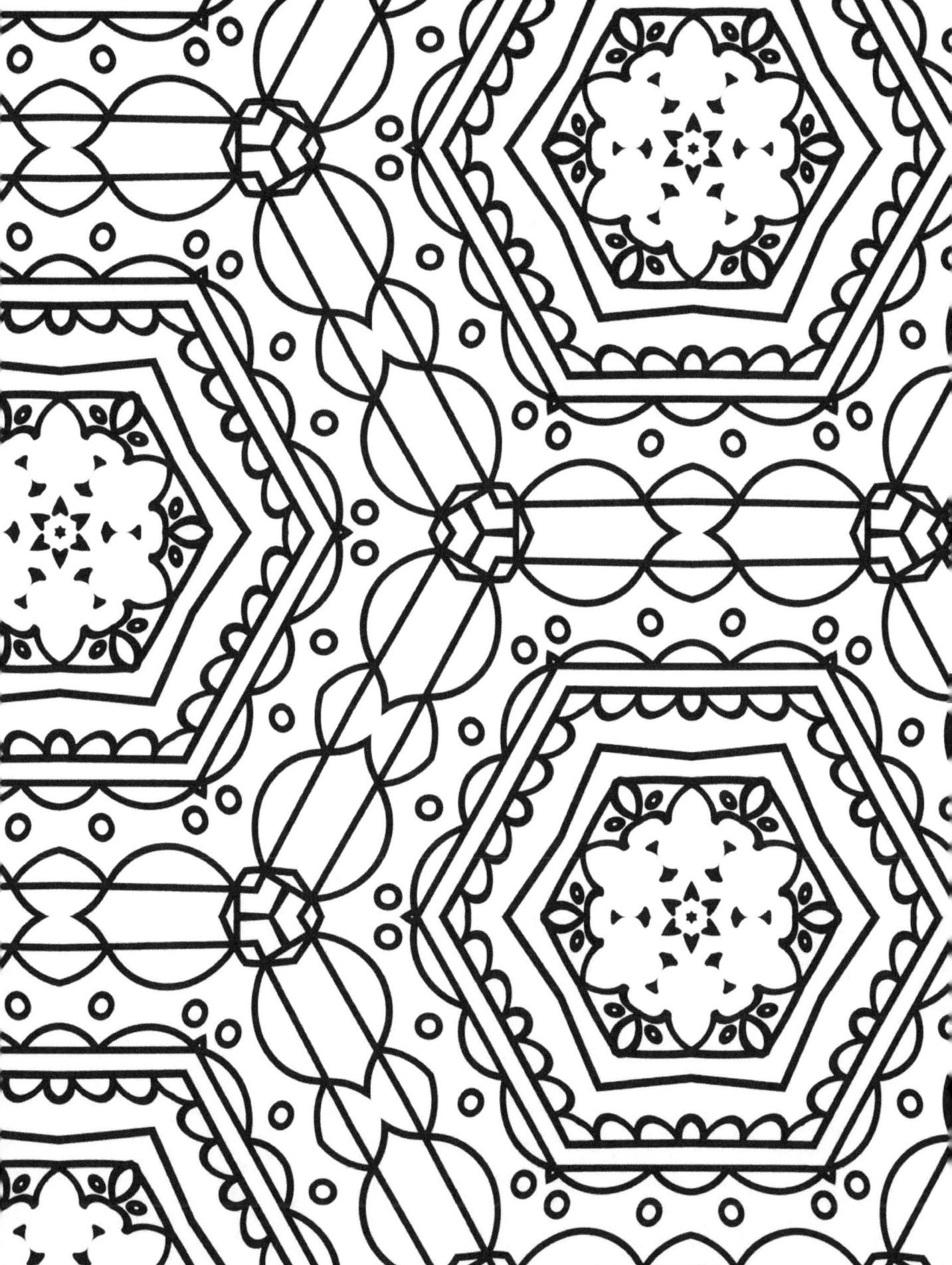

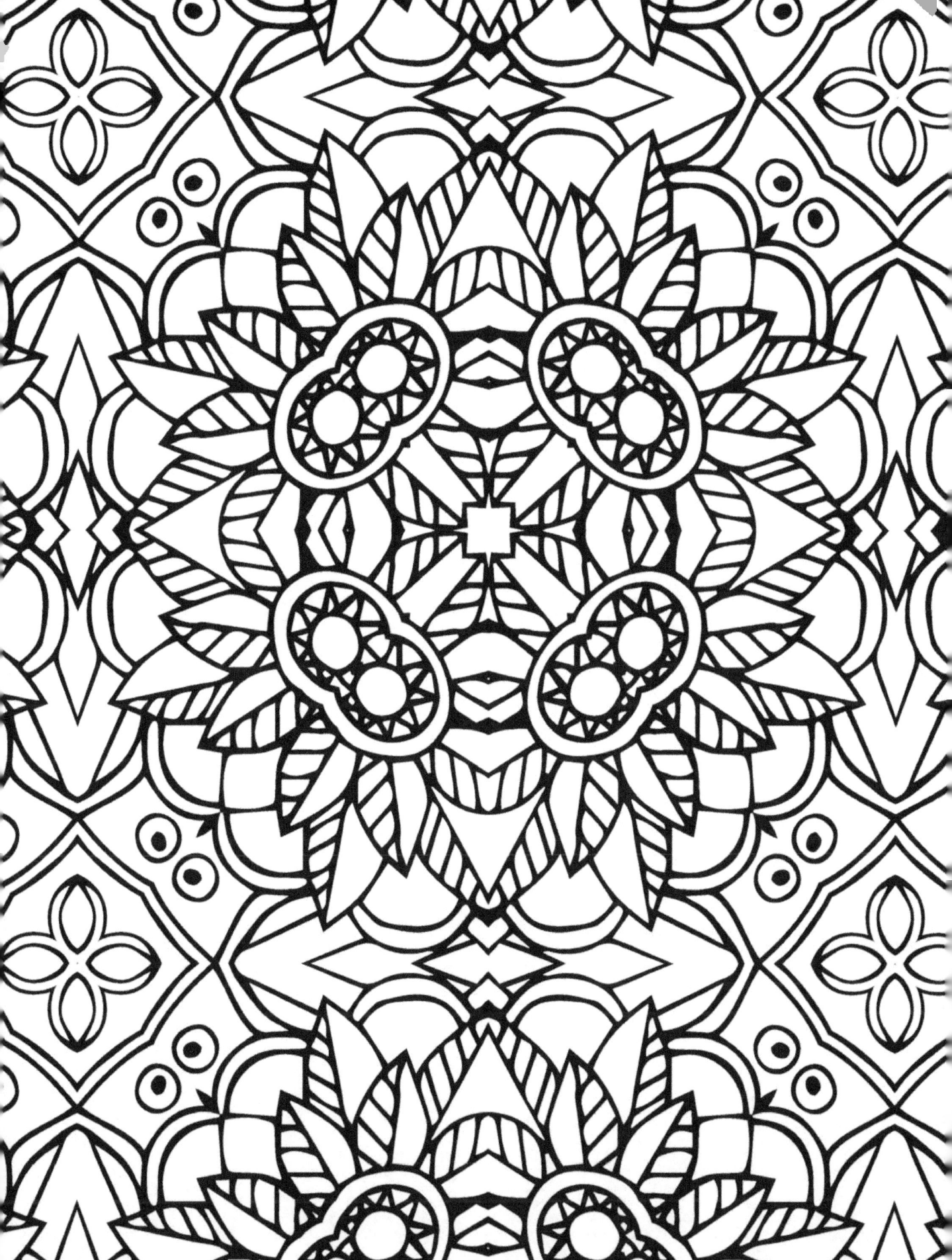

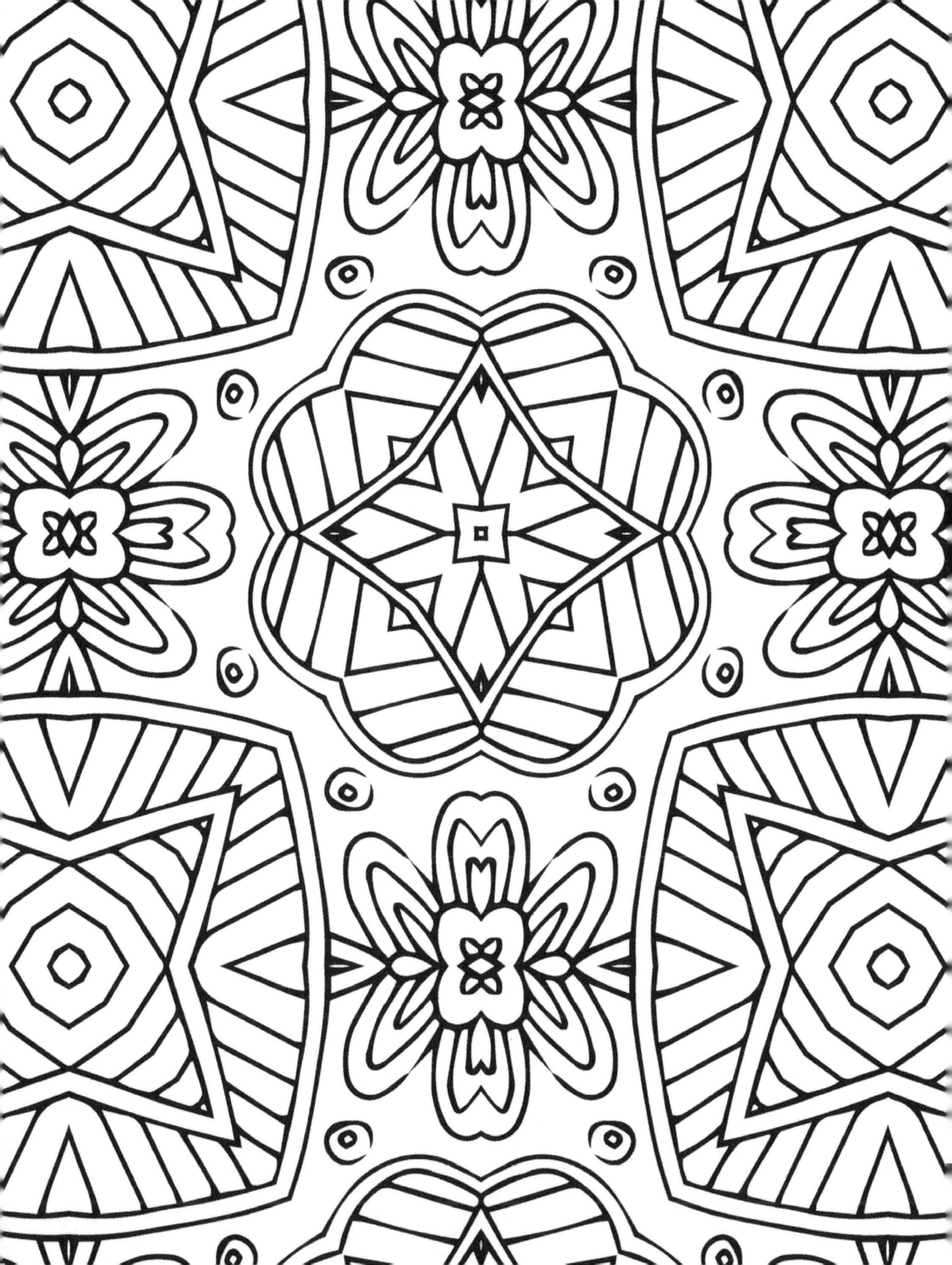

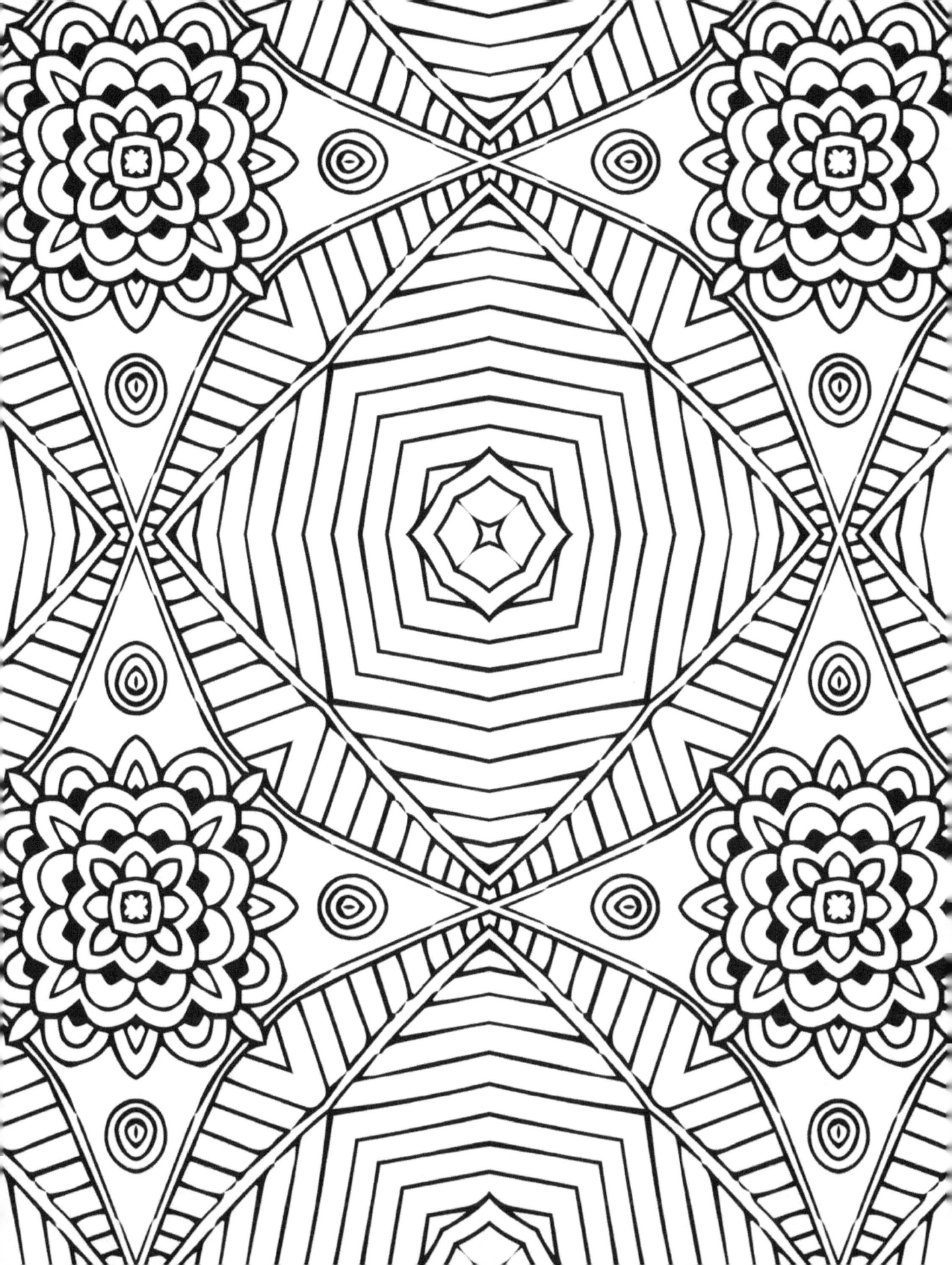

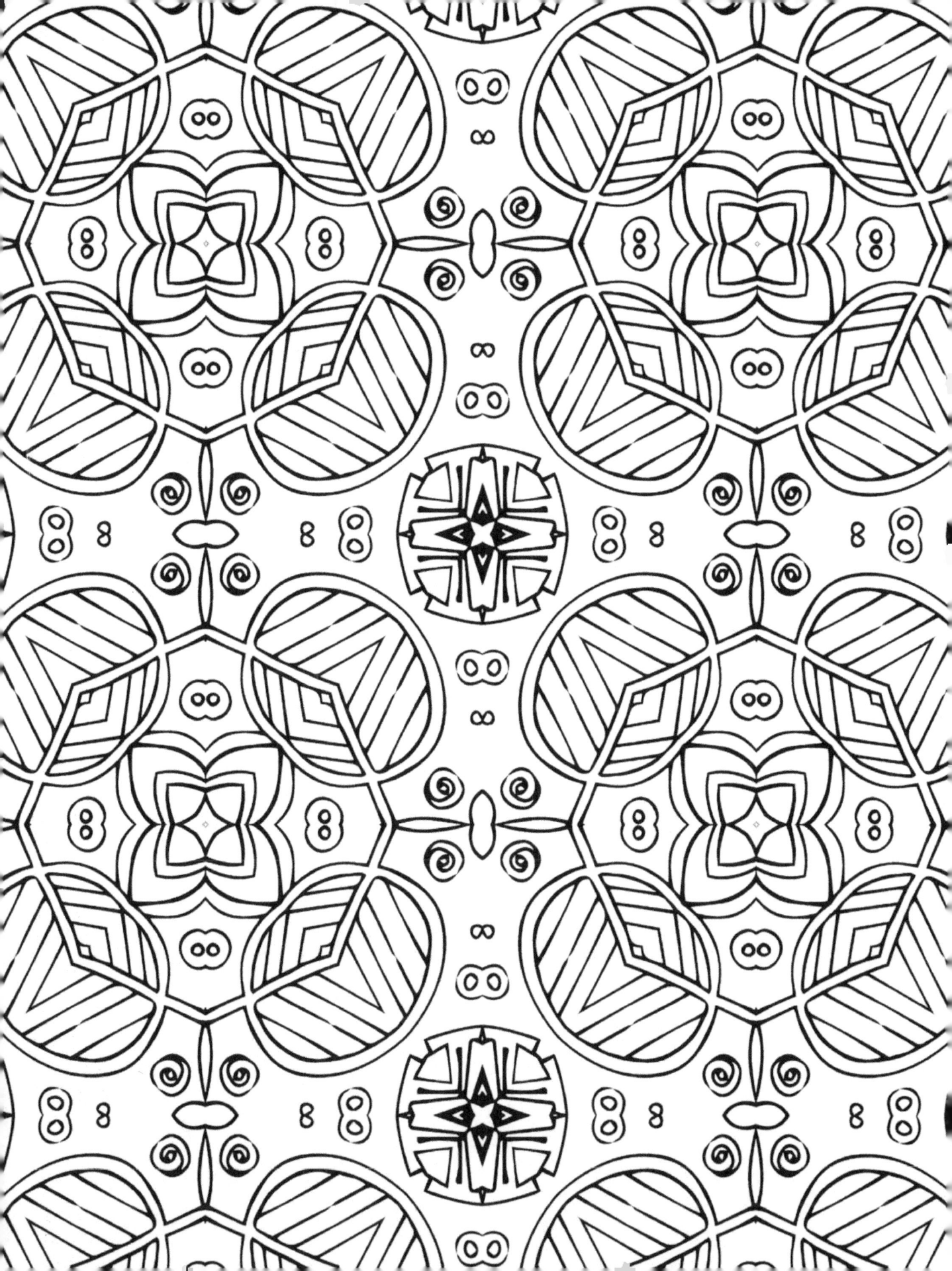

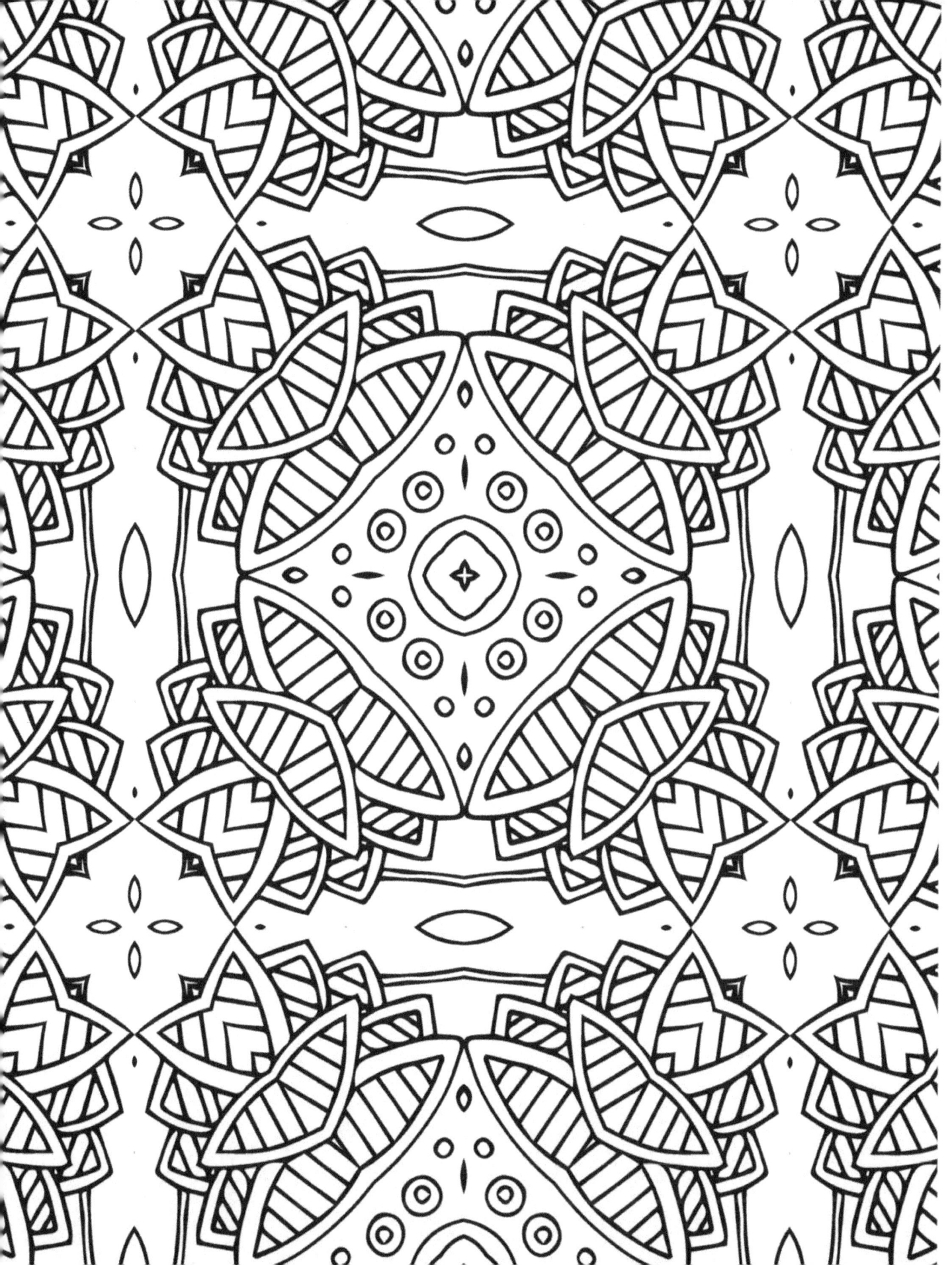

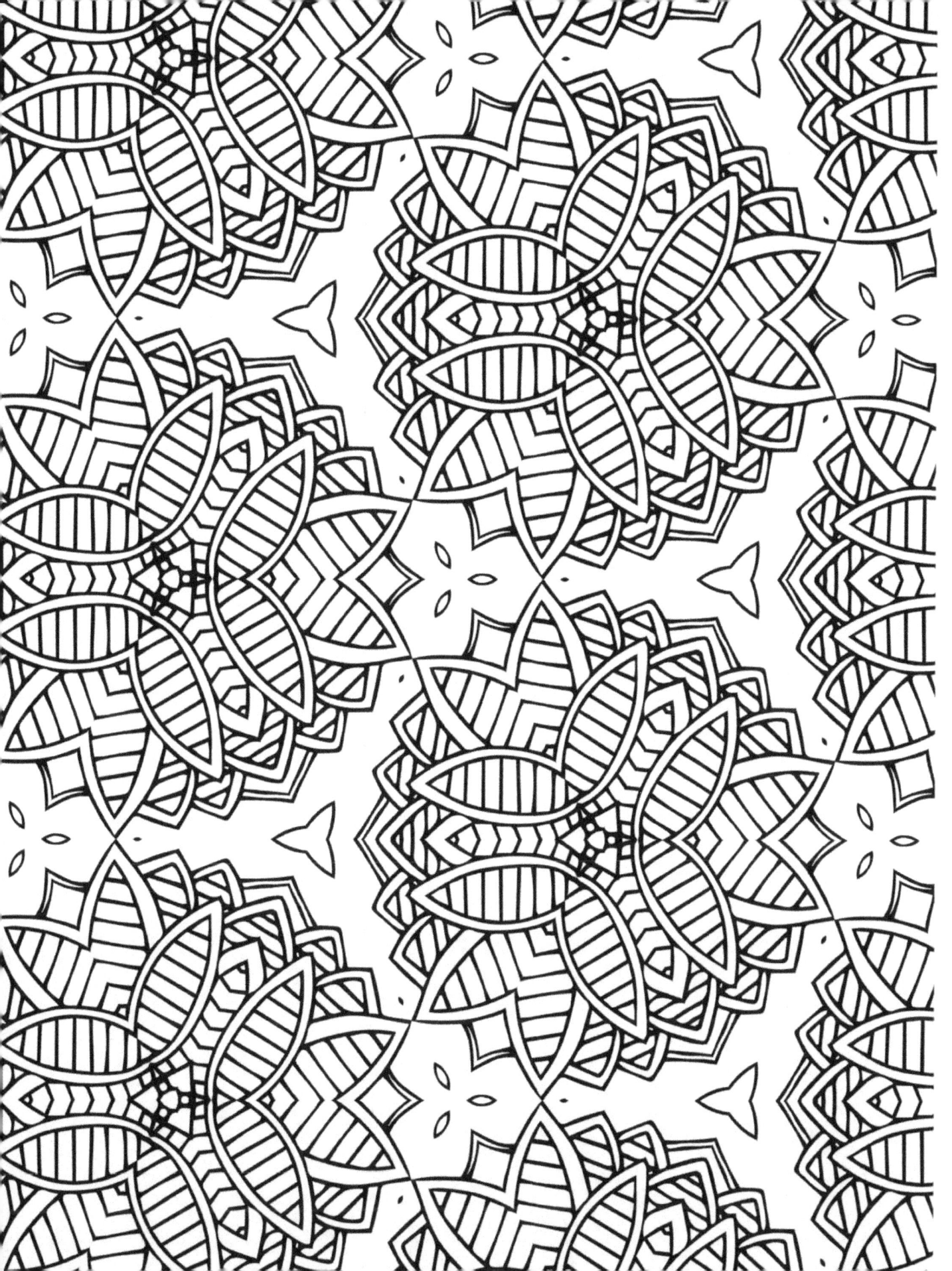

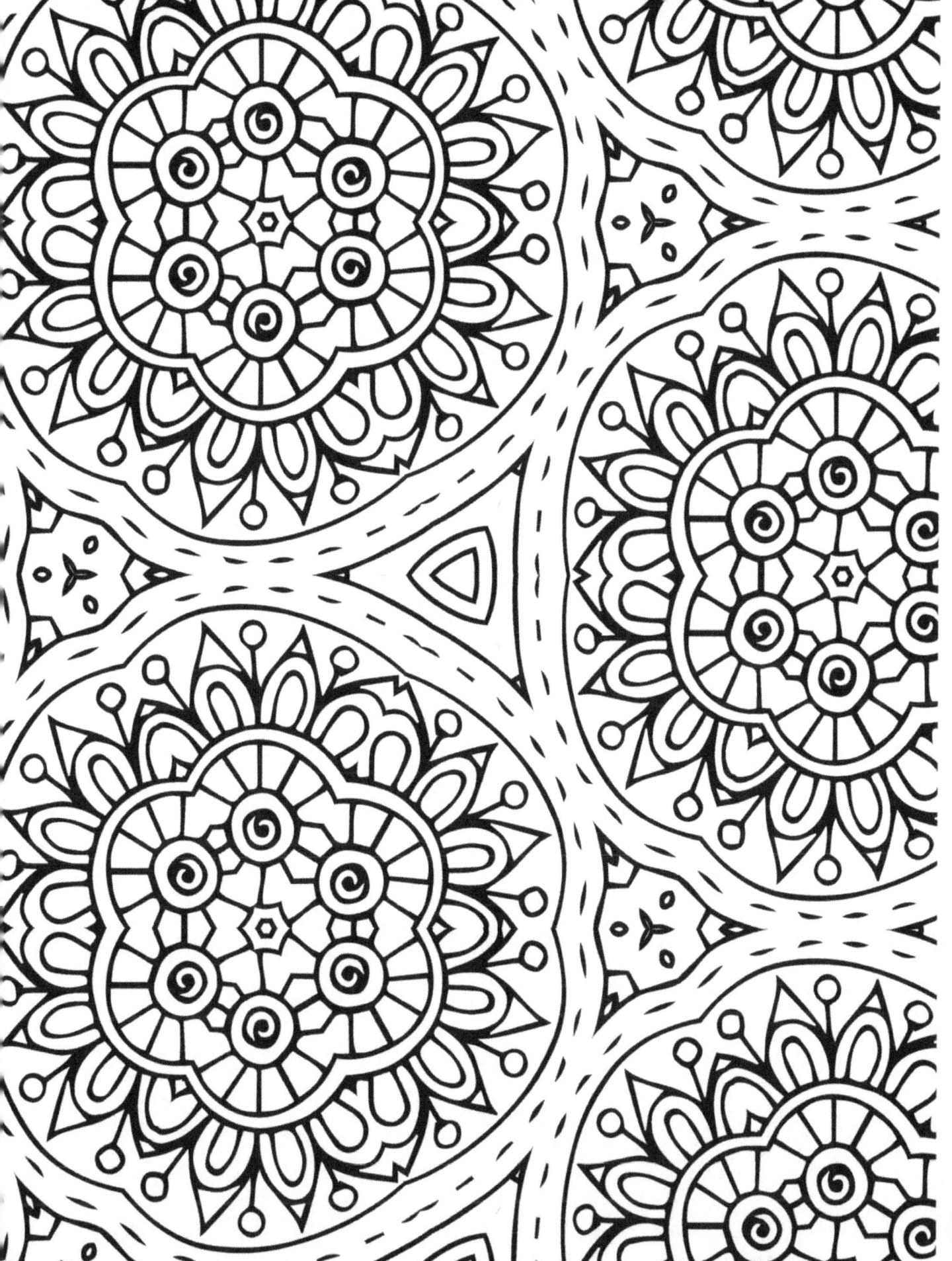

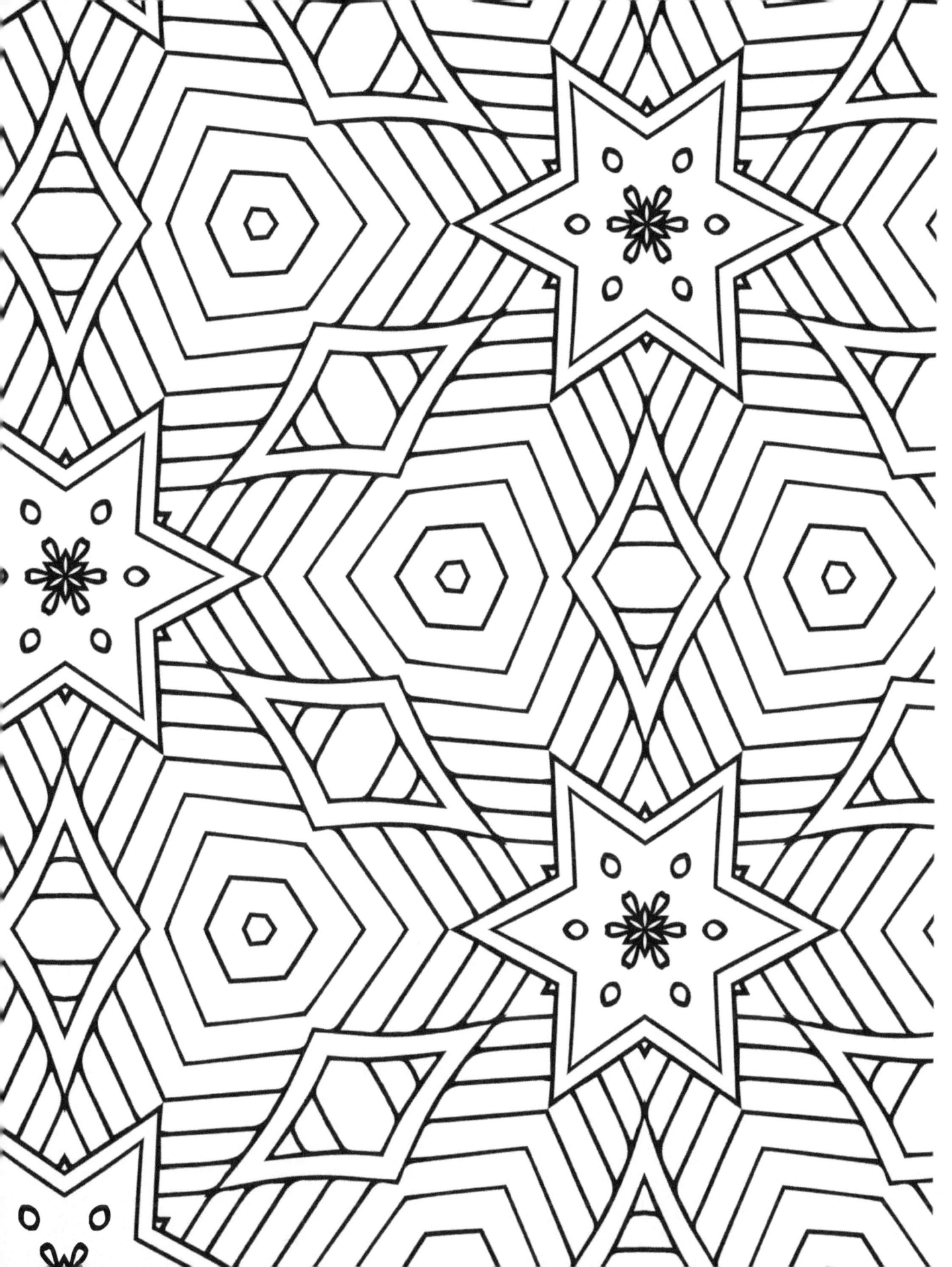

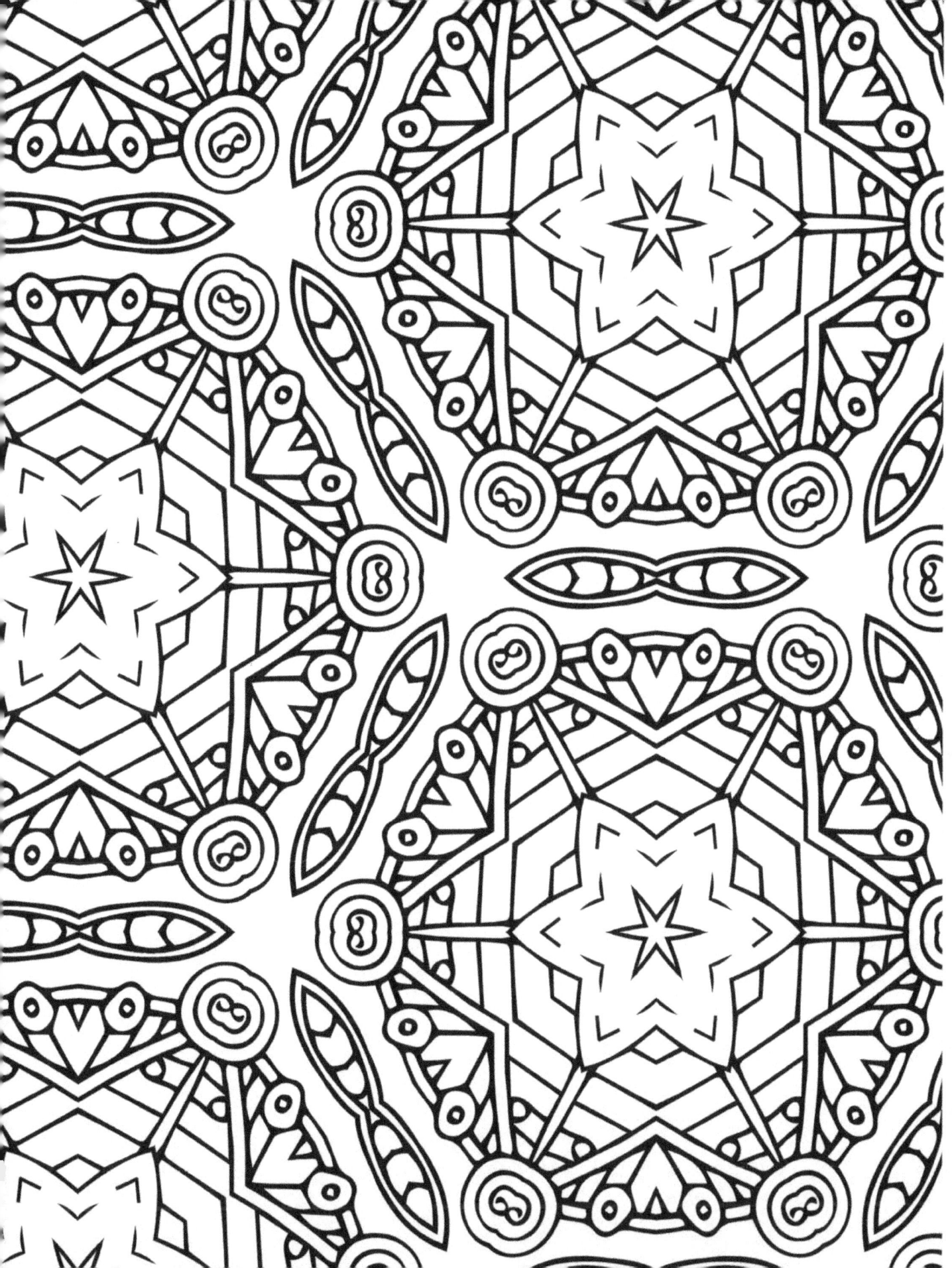

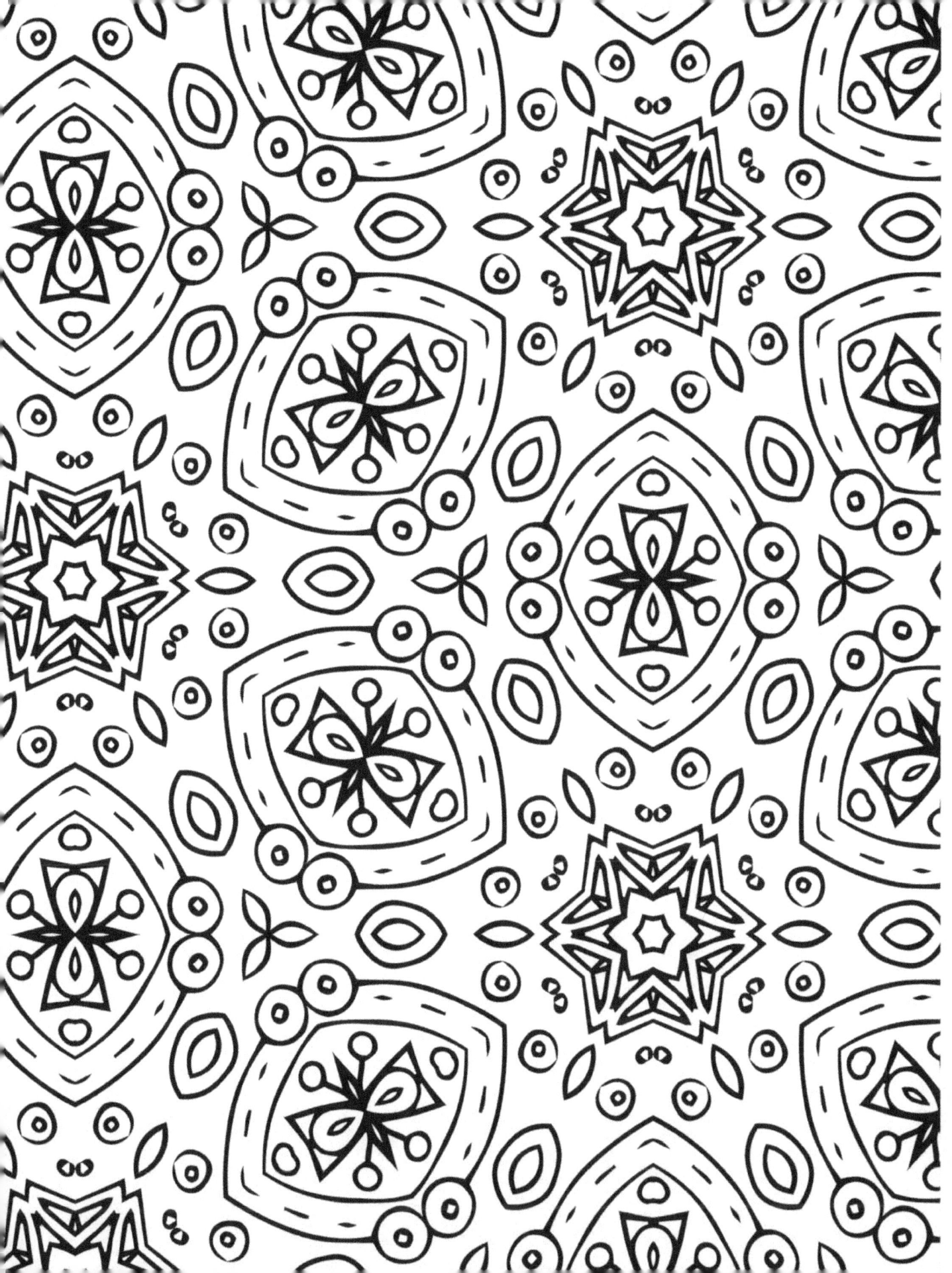

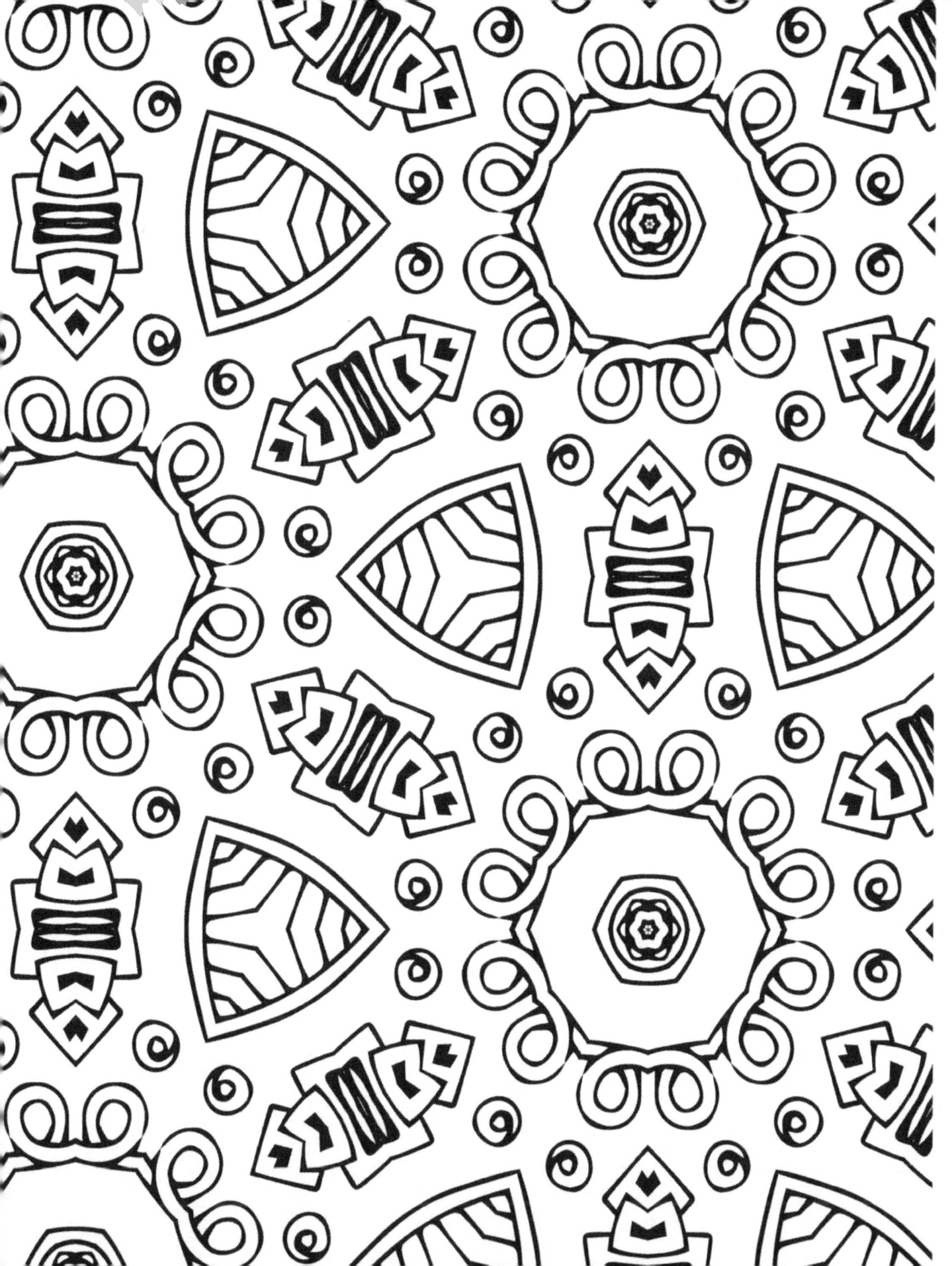

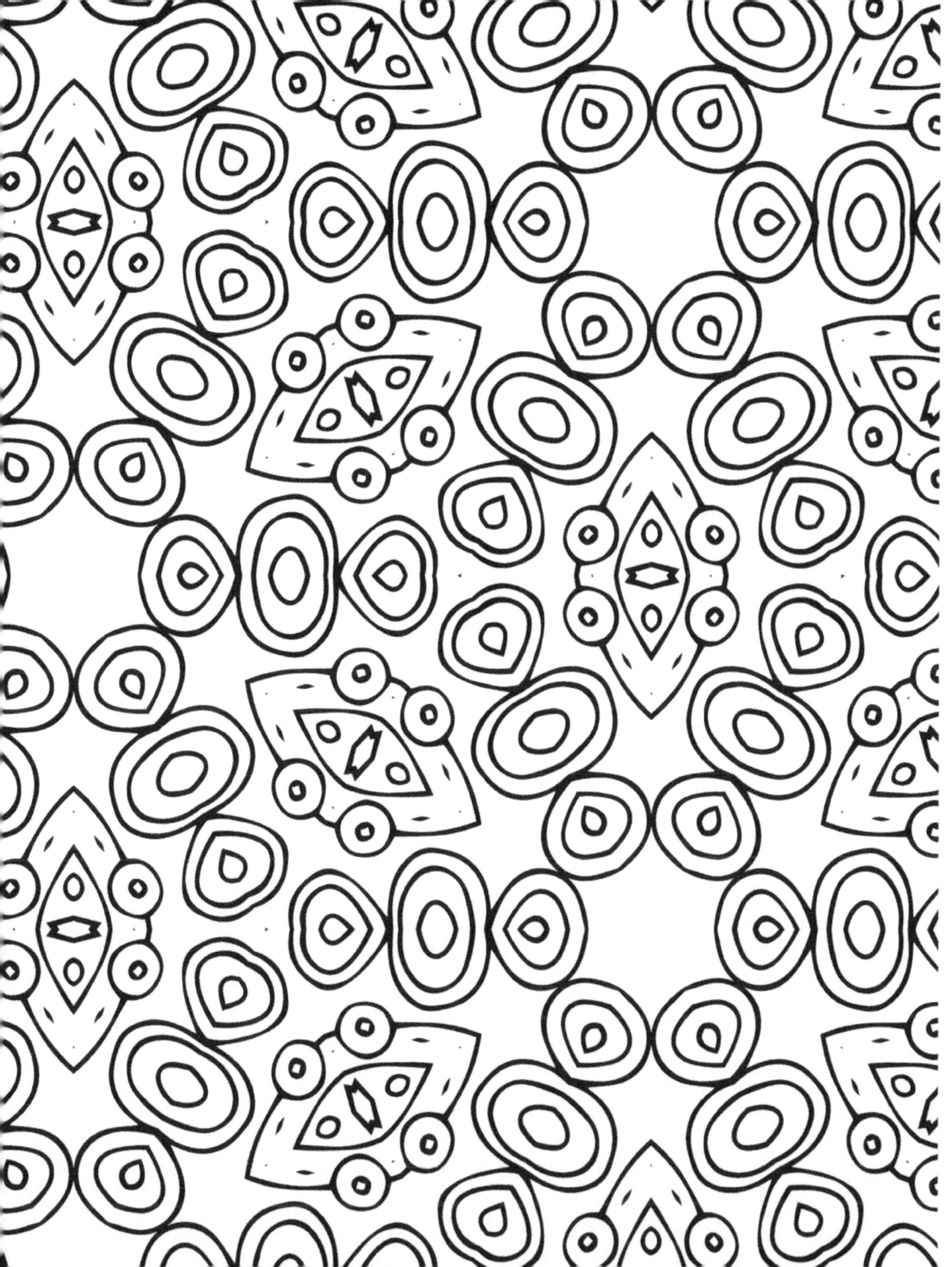

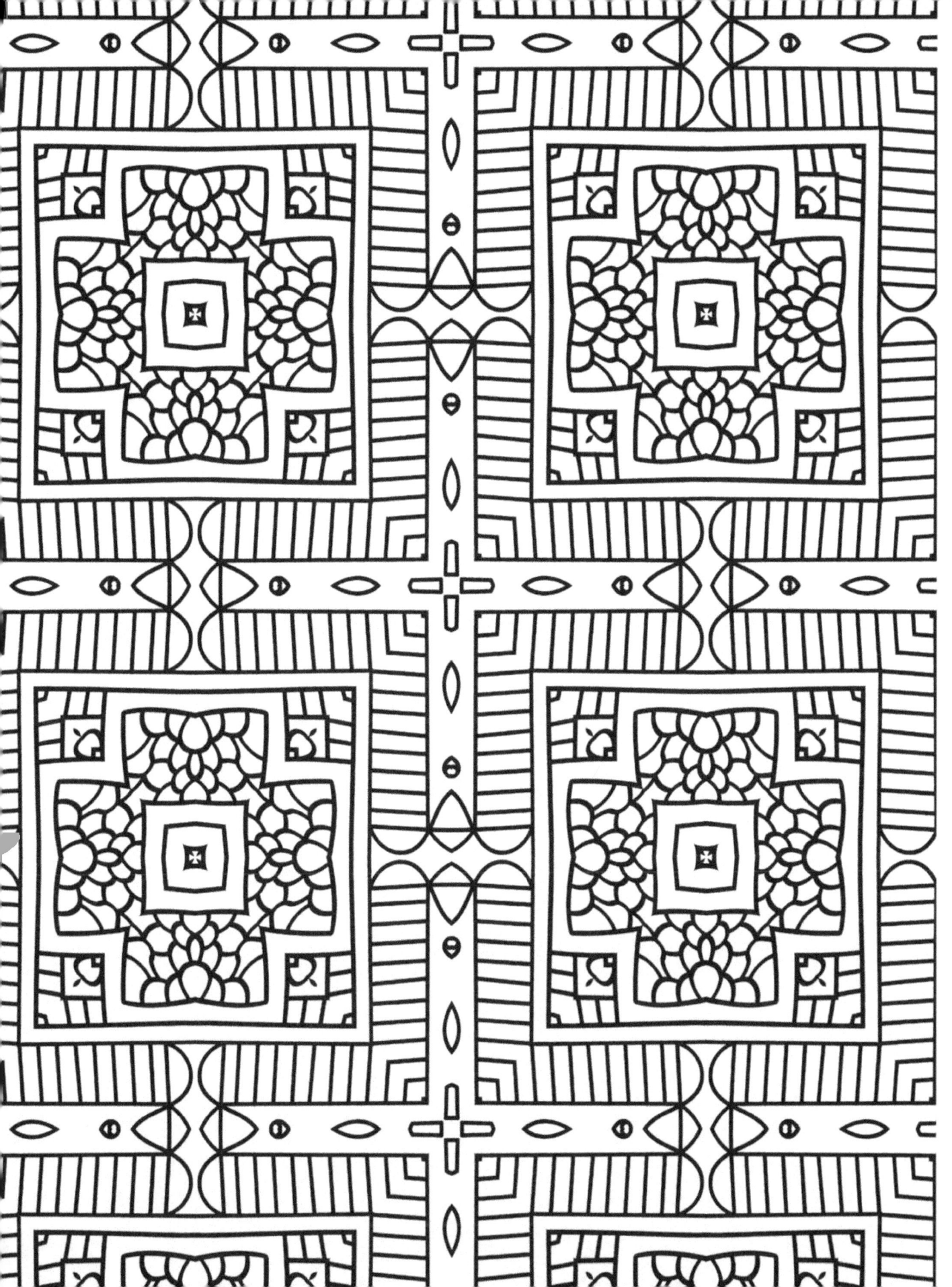